International Marketing Strategy and Export Performance

THE AUTHORS

Saad Dubayyan Alshammari holds a PhD in University Utara Malaysia. He is a Researcher at University Utara Malaysia. His main area of expertise is the international marketing and export performance. His articles have been published in a wide range of various journals. He is interested in doing research in international trade, marketing, import-export performance, tourism, migration etc.

Rabiul Islam holds a PhD in Environmental Economics under the Institute for Environment and Development at University Kebangsaan Malaysia (UKM). He is a Senior Lecturer in the Department of Economics at University Utara Malaysia. He was Post-Doctoral Fellow in Institute for Environment and Development, UKM. His main area of expertise is the application of Global Forest Products Model (GFPM). His articles have been published in a wide range of various journals. He is interested in doing research in international trade, trade and environment, tourism, migration, water, poverty and food security, urban agriculture, sustainable development, climatic hazards, and green economics.

Dr. Ahmad Bashawir Abdul Ghani is currently an Associate Professor in International Business Management with the College of Law, Government and International Studies at University Utara Malaysia, where he has taught international business for 15 years and has supervised about 10 business research projects. He holds an MBA in Financial Management from the University of Hull, UK and a PhD in Commerce from Murdoch University, Australia. His research and consultancy interests cover the theoretical and applied aspects of international business, business research, strategic alliances, strategic/policy modelling, and business economics. He has also published in a wide range of international, Australian and New Zealand journals. In addition, he has spoken at conferences throughout the world on matters dealing with international business management. Prior to joining University Utara Malaysia, he has previously worked in a number of public and private sector organizations in Malaysia and abroad, where he has been involved in economic, strategic and business research projects spanning most sectors of the economy. He is currently The Dean School of International Studies, College of Law, Government and International Studies at University Utara Malaysia.

International Marketing Strategy and Export Performance

With Special Reference to Malaysia

Saad Dubayyan Alshammari
Rabiul Islam
Ahmad Bashawir Abdul Ghani

SHIPRA

Rs. 750; US$ 37.50

ISBN: 978-81-7541-822-6

First Published in India in 2015

International Marketing Strategy and Export Performance: With Special Reference to Malaysia

Published by:
SHIPRA PUBLICATIONS
LG 18-19, Pankaj Central Market, I.P. Ext.
Patparganj, Delhi-110092, India
Tel: 91-11-2223 5152, 2223 6152
E-mail: info@shiprapublication.com
www.shiprapublication.com

Thanks to

Almighty Allah

For making this and everything possible

Preface

The study aimed at investigating the impact of the antecedent factors on the performance of exporting companies in Malaysia through the mediating influence of marketing mix adaptation.

We express our deepest appreciation to Dr. Asmat Nizam Abdul Talib and Dr. Abdul Rahim Bin Abu Bakar who have been very helpful and supportive throughout our research process. Thank you for all the help that you have provided us and your continuing patience in reviewing the countless revisions of our write up. We have learned a lot and we are totally indebted to both of you.

Our special thanks to Prince Salman bin Abdul Aziz Al Saud, Vice Custodian of the Two Holy Mosques, the Crown Prince First Deputy Prime Minister and Minister of Defence of Saudi Arabia. Prince Salman is the father of the late Prince Fahad Bin Salman who was a great support for us and who encouraged us before we started our research. We pray all the time to Almighty Allah that Prince Fahad's soul will rest in peace with all the good souls in Heavens.

Authors

Contents

One
Introduction

BACKGROUND

Over the last few years, the world has witnessed an increase in the total number of firms located in emerging economies and global markets, in countries like Brazil, China, India, and other East Asian countries, growing from just under 3,000 firms to more than 13,000 firms currently (UNCTAD, 2006).

This phenomenon stems from a comprehensive internationalization of these firms. In 2008, emerging economies contributed 38 per cent of world merchandise exports (WTO Trade Report, 2009). These emerging countries, comprising the biggest and fastest growing economies, are helping to stabilize the world economy, as a result of their dynamism and openness. For the Asian region, the contributions to world trade have been phenomenal, with a GDP expansion exceeding 6 per cent in 2007, as opposed to other regions, such as Latin America (3.7%) and Africa (3%) (UNCTAD Report, 2008). A majority of these emerging countries are achieving current account surpluses, thus becoming significant capital providers to the other countries (UNCTAD Report, 2008).

The success of emerging economies from Asia, in terms of their exports, has ignited great interest to comprehend the international marketing strategies used to enhance export performance in the Asian region (Shoham, 1996). Generally, when firms begin penetrating into a foreign market, the main step towards successful international market penetration, is the correct selection of suitable international marketing strategies to ensure adaptation to products exported (Chung, 2002). Therefore, globalization throughout the international market is significant for international marketers to understand the extent of adaptation of their products in international markets.

Countries in Southeast Asia, including Malaysia, Thailand, Vietnam, Indonesia and Philippines, are being hailed as the major players in the global market. Their firms are becoming very significant globally, and some of them have been listed as top ranking multinational firms in the world, along with multinational firms from developed countries. It is relevant to note that international trading from the Asian region contributes a total of approximately 56 per cent, which represents over half of the world trade flow (UNCTAD, 2009).

Malaysia is considered as one of those countries in Southeast Asia that has recently undergone rapid economic growth. Malaysia is considered as a model for successful economic development by many organizations, including the World Bank and the International Monetary Fund. Recently, Malaysia is regarded as one of the major trading nations in the world, ranking at seventeenth place. The Malaysian economy is dependent on external trade, and through a series of a five-year development plans, the country has been able to transform itself from a country that just exports rubber and tin, to being the world's largest exporter of palm oil products, as well as some other products, such as timber, oil and other manufactured products. A very significant point to note is that the manufacturing sector has replaced the agricultural sector in the top most spot. Today, Malaysia is also a major exporter of semi-conductors, air-conditioners and latex-dipped goods. Malaysia is acutely aware that trade plays a major role in the country's economic development and advancement.

To retain its competitiveness and its stable economy, Malaysia realizes that expansion of trade is vital for the country; therefore, Malaysia is constantly seeking for new markets for its products. However, Malaysian firms located in foreign markets face countless obstacles, as well as complicated business surroundings, including other obstacles, like environmental, legal, political, social-cultural and economic factors. These factors significantly affect a firm's marketing activities. According to Jain (1989), Theodosiou and Leonidou (2003), marketing decisions are mostly centered on issues of standardization or adaptation. These are the critical issues that have strategic implications for product adaptation, which can affect the export performance and international marketing strategy, especially for a country like Malaysia—a nation that mostly depends on exports to make significant growths in the economy.

PROBLEM STATEMENT

Regardless of the huge amount of research and ongoing debate regarding standardization/adaptation of international marketing strategy, researchers are of the consensus that many questions crucial to practitioners and researchers, are still untouched in the international marketing literature. Firstly, the determinants influencing the level of firm's adaptation appear to be scattered throughout the literature particularly in the export context. Thus, even though the findings of previous studies made the comprehension of standardization/adaptation to be instrumental, the determinants still remain unclear. The scattered information collected from the findings cannot be generalized and hence, they fail to provide a practical framework for all international marketers. Therefore, it is imperative that a study of the current studies' caliber that patches the discrepancies needs to be carried out.

Secondly, studies regarding firm's adaptation from contingency theory and from the strategy fit perspective have not received ample attention from researchers (Calantone *et al.*, 2006), despite its being one of the most prominent and evolving theories encapsulated in the international business and marketing strategy (Wernerfelt, 1984, 1995; Barney, 1991; Barney, Wright & Ketchen, 2001). According to the contingency perspective, standardization/adaptation decision is a process comprising a number of antecedent factors (Akaah, 1991; Jain, 1989; Rau & Preble, 1987). Contingency theorists claim that firm's performance greatly depends on the successful alignment or strategic fit between an organization's internal processes (strategy, structure, and resources) and the external environment (Lawrence & Lorsch 1967; Aldrich, 1979; Keats & Hitt, 1988). This particular view states that neither standardization nor adaptation can be viewed in an isolated situation and that both processes ought to be considered as the two ends that form the same continuum, upon which the level of firms' marketing strategy standardization/adaptation move between (Cavusgil, Zou & Naidu, 1993; Theodisou & Leonidou, 2003). Therefore, the challenge faced by the international firms is to pinpoint which of the strategic elements are suitable, and in which environment and up to which level. Hence, it is crucial for any research conducted in the same topic to make use of this perspective for a comprehensive understanding of standardization/adaptation issues. Calantone *et al.* (2006) explored the adaptation from this perspective but only focused on product adaptation and failed to explore other marketing mix elements; thus, some antecedents of the firm's adaptation are still unclear. This is a research gap that needs to be addressed in under to enable better comprehension and application.

Thirdly, studies dealing with the investigation of standardization/ adaptation issues concerning international marketing strategy were mostly adopted from the United States (US), Europe, Australia and New Zealand; in other words, all advanced countries in the global economy (Zou, Andrus and Novell, 1997; Chung, 2002, 2004). Hence, the findings are unsuitable for emerging countries like Malaysia. This is due to the fact that the contexts, measures and firm's characteristics of the advanced countries are quite different compared to the emerging economies. Additionally, there are other factors which contribute to the firm's behavior that have yet to be explored in studies on advanced economies. It is impossible to generalize these findings, as well as extend them to firms in emerging economies. Thus, there is a need for a study which focuses on the emerging countries to provide clearer overview of the standardization/adaptation phenomenon.

Fourthly, only a few studies have attempted to investigate the emerging countries' adaptation. Two studies were carried out in the Newly Industrialized Countries (NICs) or Korea, conducted by Han and Kim (2003) and Park (2006). The NICs are countries that developed very quickly in recent times, because of rapid industrialized development, compared to emerging economies, which are those countries presently going through a robust economic development. The distinction between both economies normally creates gaps among the firms in various aspects of the marketing programs. Therefore, the findings collected from the NICs may not be wholly suitable in its applicability to the emerging economies. Malaysia is one of the leading emerging countries in Asia and has been considered as a model for most business developments for other developing countries, particularly in Asia, the Middle East and Africa, including the Kingdom of Saudi Arabia. In 2010 and towards the end of the ninth five-year plan, Malaysia achieved 96.2 per cent of the development projects, totalling RM 230 billion, thus progressing towards Vision 2020 (FFM, 2011). Furthermore, Malaysia is a moderate Islamic country that is looked up to by many other Islamic countries, worldwide. The development and success Malaysia secured during the past two decades drew the attention of most countries in the Middle East and the Arab World. This encouraged many leaders in the Middle East to visit Malaysia to learn about its development, and even forge partnerships in different fields. An example was the visit by the Saudi King, Abdullah in 2006. The King instructed that the Malaysian example should be studied and made use of in the Arab World in general, and in Saudi Arabia, in particular, specifically the economical and industrial development. This royal visit resulted in many agreements between Saudi Arabia and Malaysia, especially in the fields of economy and education (Saudi Chamber of Commerce, 2012). Thus, it hoped that the findings of the study would provide useful data for the Saudi government especially that the government has been trying to diversify their economy resources by embarking on manufacturing and producing diverse variety of products in an attempt to put an end to the major dependence on oil.

Finally, only a limited number of researchers investigated the adaptation level of marketing mix elements on the basis of antecedent factors in the export context. This limitation created deficiencies, which in turn, created vulnerable conditions for international marketers to thrive, and expand their business globally. Empirical findings can contribute accurate evidence for newcomers, for e.g., firms from emerging countries in the global market, in the face of stiff global competition. A deep comprehension regarding the antecedent factors in the export context would likely lead to successful exporting activities. For this to be realized, there is a need for more studies to be carried out in order to provide a better understanding of the antecedent factors that influence export performance, in the context of standardization/adaptation.

Owing to the limited number of studies regarding international marketing and business literature, there exists no clear benchmark for international marketers to find the adaptation level of the marketing mix on the basis of the complex conditions of the international markets (Cavusgil, Zou & Naidu, 1993). Despite the constant growth of emerging countries in the global economy, only limited information regarding marketing strategies reach the international marketers from these emerging countries. Hence, they are open to intense competition from both multinational and domestic companies (Han & Kim, 2003). This further reveals the gap in literature in this area, which this study attempts to fill.

The study regarding emerging economies is imperative for the comprehension of the relationship between international marketing strategy/ adaptation and its antecedents in two important aspects: (1) firms in emerging countries possess less information regarding the export market conditions compared to the firms in the western world. This is the reason why marketers from the West are capable of making effective decisions regarding the standardization or adaptation of their international marketing strategy. In sum, the relationship that exists between standardization/adaptation and various conditions may be more accurate for Western firms as compared to their counterparts in the emerging countries; (2) firms have always extended their local marketing strategy to foreign markets without making modifications (Douglas & Craig, 1989). Following years of industrialization, Malaysian firms have transformed into one of the major countries in the world in different product categories, like semi-conductors, furniture, home appliances, etc. Nonetheless, the study attempts to investigate whether emerging countries' firms, such as Malaysian firms, modify (standardizing/adapting) their strategies for international markets.

Most of the research on the adaptation/standardization processes and their impact on export performance, are focused on two main streams: (1) a number of research studies investigated the impact of the antecedent factors on the market mix strategies (Park, 2006; Kim & Cavusgil, 2009); and (2) other research studies attempted to investigate the relationship between the market mix strategies and export performance (Dess, Pinkham & Yang, 2011; *Tantong*, Karande, Nair & Singhapakdi, 2010; Solomon, Marshall & Stuart, 2008). However, no studies thus far, attempted to investigate the relationship between the antecedent factors and the export performance through the mediating influence of market mix strategies. This link between the antecedent factors and the export performance through the mediating influence of market mix strategies, is the contribution of this study to literature in this area.

More importantly, during the past two decades, the Malaysian exporting firms have been experiencing tremendous challenges in securing competitive advantage in the international market due to the open policy of highly competitive countries like China, Taiwan and South Korea. In this context, Maheran (2008) argues that the emergence of low cost producers and manufacturing policies in countries like China and South Korea intensified the competitiveness of the Malaysia exporting activities. Maheran (2008) goes on to say that one of problems Malaysian exporters have is that they do not adopt adaptation policies to their products and exporting activities and even the little level of adaptation being practiced by some Malaysian exporters is not even grounded on thorough understanding and investigation of the nature of the host markets.

RESEARCH OBJECTIVES

In order to bridge the gap in existing literature as mentioned above, the current study explores the antecedent factors that have been hypothesized to affect the marketing mix, and in turn, the export performance of the Malaysian firms. In other words, taken from a general view, the current study aims to explore the degree of the firm's adaptation in their marketing program and export performance, in the light of products and services adaptation in the foreign or host market. More importantly, this study attempts to examine the relationship between the antecedent factors and the export performance through the mediating influence of market mix strategies.

Thus, the present research attempts to achieve the following objectives:

1. To find out the effect of the antecedent factors on the degree of adaptation of the marketing mix in the Malaysian export companies;
2. To examine the impact of the antecedent factors on the performance of Malaysian export companies through the mediating effect of marketing mix; and.
3. To examine the impact of the level of marketing mix strategy adaptation on the performance of Malaysian export companies.

RESEARCH CONTRIBUTION

The current research generally contributes to both the international marketing and international business strategy, and these contributions can be divided into three perspectives, as discussed below:

1. *Theoretical Contribution:* A close look at the literature review shows that several previous studies regarding international standardization and adaptation focused on understanding the underlying theories on international marketing. Likewise, this study contributes to the comprehension of standardization/adaptation from the perspective of the contingency view and strategy fit approach. Studies concerning marketing mix elements exploring the same view are few and far between. Therefore, this study explores literatures on these theories.

Additionally, this study makes it possible for firms to pinpoint key antecedent factors from the literature that have the greatest possibility of affecting the level of marketing program adaptation in the export markets. Moreover, this study provides a clear relationship between the key determinants and the degree of marketing mix, which in turn, helps lay the basis of measurement for international marketers to determine the level of program adaptation in the international markets.

In addition, in the present research, marketing mix adaptation is considered as a function of firms' factors or referred to as antecedent factors. These factors include international experience, technology intensity, competition level, government regulation, cultural differences, economic differences, country image, physical condition, and marketing infrastructure. More importantly, as mentioned earlier, most of the research studies on the adaptation/standardization processes, and their impact on export performance, focused on two main streams. In the first stream, a number of research studies investigated the impact of the antecedent factors on the market mix strategies (Park, 2006; Kim & Cavusgil, 2009). In the second stream, other research studies attempted to investigate the relationship between the market mix strategies and export performance (Dess, Pinkham & Yang, 2011; Tantong, Karande, Nair & Singhapakdi, 2010; Solomon, Marshall & Stuart, 2008). However, no studies thus far have explored the relationship between the antecedent factors and the export performance through the mediating influence of market mix strategies. The latter link between the antecedent factors and the export performance through the mediating influence of market mix strategies, is the contribution of this study, besides filling the gap in the literature.

More importantly, most of the previous work examined the influence of the antecedent factors on the marketing mix strategies individually. In other words, the impact of each antecedent factor was examined on each of the marketing mix strategies. No studies attempted to examine the impact of the antecedent factors on the marketing mix as a whole. In this context, Lages (2001) argued that "it is necessary for marketers to develop a measure that looks into the marketing mix as a whole". This study responds to this call by dealing with the marketing mix as a whole construct.

2. *Managerial Contribution*: Several studies, covering international standardization/adaptation, are a response to the request from advanced countries, like from the US, Europe and Australia/New Zealand (Cavusgil, Zou and Naidu, 1993; Chung, 2003, 2006, 2009). This study provides the guidelines that will assist international marketers in the Asian context, specifically to firms located in emerging countries, with regards to international marketing strategy.

3. *Practical Contribution*: Generally speaking, international standardization and adaptation have recognized economic, political and social-cultural factors as necessary imperative external factors. These factors are increasingly affecting international standardization and adaptation of firms from emerging economies, and need to be constantly examined to offer the countries a way to better their business environment, besides providing practical experience to the countries concerned. These much needed studies could lay the basis for international marketing managers when they evaluate future business prospects and desirability for global expansion. This study assists the policy makers of emerging countries in the business development aspect, as the Malaysian experience has been considered as the model specifically for Muslim nations. The current study reveals some interesting facts that will be invaluable for Malaysian policymakers in the light of regulations concerning manufacturing and exporting activities, as well as assist other countries' policymakers to tackle their export and international trade policies.

Furthermore, it was mentioned earlier that Malaysia has been looked up to by many Islamic countries worldwide and most of the countries in the Middle East and the Arab world, as a role model for successful development. It is hoped, therefore that the findings generated from the present research would provide the Saudi managers and policy makers, a platform to learn from the Malaysian example and probably transfer some of the valuable experiences that Malaysia has gone through to their own contexts.

SCOPE

The study is limited within the parameter of Malaysian firms, which are regarded as one of the fastest developing and growing emerging economies located in the Southeast Asia region. Comprehensive information surrounding these Malaysian firms was collected with the help of a Malaysian government agency, i.e., Malaysian Trade (MATRADE), under the auspices of the Ministry of International Trade and Industry (MITI). A majority of the Malaysian firms that carry out exporting activities are registered with MATRADE, for the purpose of obtaining certain facilities and incentives. Therefore, it is the most convenient and suitable source to collect the firms' database.

The 780 targeted firms are located in three main regions, namely Selangor State, Penang State, and Sabah State. Specifically, 383 firms were from Selangor State, 247 firms were from Penang State, and finally 150 firms were from Sabah State. 401 firms responded to the questionnaire and full questionnaires were collected back. Specifically, 217 questionnaires were collected from Selangor State, 98 questionnaires were collected from Penang State, and finally 86 questionnaires were collected from Sabah State. Export managers and general managers constituted the targeted sample. The whole process of data collection took four months where it started in May until August, 2012.

Two

Literature Review

This chapter reviews the literature on international marketing standardization and export marketing strategy and is divided into four major parts: (1) literature review about standardization, adaptation and contingency approach of international marketing strategy; (2) literature review about export marketing strategy; (3) identification of various internal and external constraints of the adaptation of the marketing mix; (4) key determinants and research hypotheses.

OVERVIEW OF INTERNATIONAL MARKETING STRATEGY

Taking into account how globalized the current market is, companies have viewed the process of internationalization of their activities as a technique to keep up with the competition and secure good competitive advantage. The process of decision-making related to the international marketing mix has become a serious issue, particularly as this arrangement has a great deal of impact on performance. Consequently, a number of researchers argue that the research that relates standardization and adaptation to the performance of companies, particularly to export performance activities is highly needed (Calantone, Cavusgil, Schmidt & Shin, 2004; Julian & O'Cass, 2004; Shoham, 2002; Dow, 2006).

However, the literature concerning the best decision whether to adapt or standardize is still inconclusive, taking into account the nature of influence (positive or negative) of the two processes of standardization and adaptation have on export performance. While some researchers found that there is no relationship between these two processes and performance (Samiee & Roth, 1992), others, on the other hand, found that a positive link between the adaptation of the product and its performance does exist. Thus, the consensus among researchers on the effects of the two processes of standardization and adaptation on performance represents a gap in the literature.

A review of the literature reveals that marketing mix elements form part of the export marketing strategy. However, the components comprising an export marketing strategy have come across in literature. According to Cavusgil and Kirpalani (1993) export marketing strategy comprises of product, promotion, distribution and marketing capability. Export marketing strategy is considered as the conventional marketing plan consisting of pricing, promotion, distribution and product (Cavusgil & Zou, 1993). Some researchers like Cooper and Kleischmidt (1985) state that export marketing is considered as the product adaptation policy coupled with the market selection. Taking the perspective further, De Luz (1993) claims that export strategy consists of the four marketing mix elements, along with factors like quality control, management motivation, international business training, marketing research, target nations, competitive pricing, standardization of product and direct distribution. On the other hand, Koh and Robicheaux (1988) insist that export marketing variables comprises of product modification; export pricing compared to the US market, currency, dealer, brand name and channel strategies.

Additionally, Stewart and McAuley (2000) insist that export marketing strategy includes five aspects namely market scope, the degree of product adaptation, the degree of promotional adaptation, the level of support given to the foreign distribution channel and pricing strategy. In another similar research, Abby and Slater (1989) reveal that export marketing strategy encompasses market selection, product, pricing, promotion and distribution and Chetty and Hamilton (1993) provides that an export marketing strategy includes market selection, use of intermediaries, product mix, product development, promotion, pricing and staffing. In yet another study, Zou and Stan (1998) assert that product adaptation, product strength, promotion adaptation, promotion intensity, price adaptation, competitive pricing, channel relationships and type of channels all comprise an export marketing strategy. On the other hand, marketing program is considered as the different facets of the marketing mix like product, price, distribution and promotion (Theodosiou & Leonidou, 2003; Chung, 2007). This study examines marketing mix elements in firms exporting strategy comprising of product, promotion, distribution and pricing.

Over time, scholars have established that all firms ought to adapt to their surroundings, markets, or environments for them to succeed. All firms subsist in particular social, physical, cultural, and technological environments, to which they ought to adapt (Solomon, Marshall & Stuart, 2008). Earlier researches were inclined towards ignoring or under-estimating the significance of environment-firm linkages (Kotabe & Helsen, 2009; Peng, 2011; Zou, Kim & Cavusgil, 2009). Appreciating the interdependence, significance, and complexity that underlie the linkages, leads to an understanding that firms should be viewed in their larger environmental contexts. Failing to evaluate their environment occasions the risk of zeroing in on some of the environmental characteristics, at the expense of numerous others (Dekkers, 2009; Devinney, Pedersen & Tihanyi, 2010).

In the case of firms that have international operations but are domiciled in emerging nations, they face marked challenges with respect to the actuality that they ought to adapt concurrently to the varied global environments in which they carry out their operations (Solomon, Marshall & Stuart, 2008). Regardless of the significance of appreciating the firms' environments, quite a few researches have been conducted in relation to the summative Global Business Environment (GBE), and a few researches on the firms' adaptation to the GBE (Hieu & Truong, 2010; Javalgi & Todd, 2011; Kiss, Danis & Cavusgil, 2011). When one looks up the term 'adaptation' in databases of business-related articles, the result would be quite few articles bearing that term (Kotabe & Helsen, 2009; Peng, 2011; Zou, Kim & Cavusgil, 2009).

A review of GBE related literature shows that none of the available research adequately addresses GBE's complexity, or describes why firms, especially from emerging economies, should adapt to it (Hieu & Truong, 2010; Javalgi & Todd, 2011; Kiss, Danis & Cavusgil, 2011). One can reasonably postulate that the varied environments are characterized as fundamental determinants of the firms' success. In wide-ranging literature, the environments are treated in manners that are non-operational, vague and non-precise. Most researches project the environments as sets of factors that define the firms' operations, and that they are uncontrollable (Dekkers, 2009; Devinney, Pedersen & Tihanyi, 2010). Most researches limit their evaluations to partial dimensions, like cultural discrepancies, differentials in exchange rates, incentives from governments, diversity of income-related profiles, and disparities in legal systems, amongst others. While these elements are important, they do adequately capture GBE's complexity, and importance, consequently missing the worth that is otherwise lent by adaptation to the firms' central competitive advantages. Thus, the GBE is projected as being an extensive factor, presenting firms with varied opportunities along with challenges (Ahlstrom & Bruton, 2010; Jain & Griffith, 2011; Peng, 2009).

A number of sources concern themselves with establishing whether firms from emerging economies, which are in export businesses, employ global adaptation strategies or standardization (Ahlstrom & Bruton, 2010; Jain & Griffith, 2011; Solomon, Marshall & Stuart, 2008). Most researches indicate that a product's type strongly influences whether a firm will employ an adaptation strategy or will employ standardization. High-tech exports have a high likelihood of being linked to the standardization strategy as opposed to the adaptive strategy. Industrial merchandises are commonly marketed via a standardized approach as opposed to an adaptive one. Consumer merchandises' marketing will usually be conducted through an adaptive one. Among the subsets of consumer merchandises, durables are largely and easily marketed via standardized approaches or strategy.

The nondurables, generally, have their marketing done via adaptive approaches. Particularly, offerings of food are limited to adaptive strategies (Dekkers, 2009; Devinney, Pedersen & Tihanyi, 2010). Some firms shape their strategies in ways that facilitate, support, and firm their direct exportation of products. Direct exportation has been shown to confer varied benefits to the firms: 1) the firms get substantial or complete control over any plans that they have with regard to foreign marketing (Ahmed & Rock, 2012; He & Wei, 2011). The plans may relate to product services, distribution, promotion, pricing, or others; 2) they easily focus their efforts relating to marketing on their particular product lines (Solomon, Marshall & Stuart, 2008); 3) they get quicker and more feedback and communications from the markets they are targeting. The feedback is useful to enhance the efforts of marketing with closer adaptation of products, or pricing regimens that are more responsive (Luo, Liu & Xue, 2009; Mesquita & Lazzarini, 2008; Salavou & Halikias, 2008); 4) firms get more safeguards for their intangible properties, goodwill, patents as well as trademarks. It is clear that the four benefits are only actualized when the firms that export products are wholly responsible for their efforts in global marketing, and in executing their entry strategies.

Whenever a firm settles on distributors or agents as the most convenient, cost-effective, and profitable channel of export, it ought to commence a process of screening to select the best of the possible distributors, manufacturers, or agents (Kotabe & Helsen, 2009; Peng, 2011; Zou, Kim & Cavusgil, 2009). To enter a target market in a foreign nation, a firm from the emerging world may choose to engage the services of global trading companies, export merchants, foreign-resident buyers, allied producers or manufacturers, companies for managing exports, foreign distributors or agents, foreign subsidiaries or branches, retailing wholesalers, governments, or industrial type of users. To enter the home markets, firms may elect to engage those who distribute products to household type of consumers (Solomon, Marshall & Stuart, 2008).

Finding the most convenient, cost-effective, and profitable foreign agents along with distributors is indeed very challenging. It demands appreciable effort and attention from the firms or manufacturers (Chattopadhyay & Ozsomer, 2012; Cavusgil & Michigan State University, 2009). In screening them, two aspects have to be considered: 1) their distribution profiles; and 2) their distribution prospects. Firms may enter global markets by investing in them. In this regard, the investing firms can be extractive, market, or sourcing type of firms. The market type takes investments as modes of entering foreign markets (Dekkers, 2009; Devinney, Pedersen & Tihanyi, 2010).

The likelihood of an effectual entry through investments can be heightened in varied ways, such as utilizing the experiences attained via exporting to the target markets. Such experiences reduce the principal uncertainty that typifies the decisions for entering through the making of investments (Solomon, Marshall & Stuart, 2008). Such uncertainty may concern the potential of the market to take in sales by the firms. The investments that can be transferred to other markets or economies include finances, and skills of a marketing, technical, or other nature. Sources show that social-level type of institutions shapes the adaptive strategies of firms in varying, and complex ways (Doole & Lowe, 2008; Zou & Fu, 2011).

Societal, political, and legal changes within emerging economies affect local, as well as international firms, in relation to how they compete within and outside the economies. Some of the economies, like India, have experienced phenomenal expansions in recent times. The Indian economy has seen lots of growth in its IT sector, and in the related products along with services (Solomon, Marshall & Stuart, 2008). Boundaries that demarcated software, business processes, and software are continually being blurred. Now, the term IT appears to be quite limiting. It has gradually given way to Business Process Outsourcing (BPO).

The IT or BPO firms in emerging economies have continued to grow, with explanations of their growth focusing on the IT or BPO industry, as well as views that are based on extant resources, that emphasize the industry's nature. Notably, the industry's work may be executed offsite. The explanations are also focused on particular firms' capabilities, especially firms that desirably combine excellent skills and low cost operations (Doole & Lowe, 2008; Zou & Fu, 2011). While such explanations are largely insightful, they fail to project wholesome pictures. Explanations that are based on institutions and related factors would provide pointers to societal, legal and political changes within the institutions (Solomon, Marshall & Stuart, 2008).

Changes that are based on institutions include governments' investment in advanced education of considerable populations. These explanations are related to institutions commonly probing the varied regulatory and legal reforms, which have been actualized, leading to more and more liberalization of the emerging economies (Kotabe & Helsen, 2009; Peng, 2011; Zou, Kim & Cavusgil, 2009). Some of such economies have had reforms that have enabled entrepreneurial or business environs that are open, and competitive. Beyond the emerging economies, the larger GBE that favors globalization of firms' operations has also existed. Even then, owing to changing political realities the growing profitability of the firms from emerging economies is criticized in advanced economies (Dekkers, 2009; Devinney, Pedersen & Tihanyi, 2010). In some advanced economies, there have been efforts to bar the firms from entering them, or getting public contracts. Informally, displaced workers, unionists, journalists, and politicians have expressed reservations against the entry of the firms and often call for protectionist systems, or actions. Even then, businesses that are domiciled within the advanced economies are continually appreciating the firms' work, in terms of its value and quality (Solomon, Marshall & Stuart, 2008). Moreover, the businesses have appreciably invested in emerging countries, with some of their work being carried out by their subsidiaries, which share the pools of talents that they draw personnel from with the firms. The entry of the businesses in the emerging nations has compelled the firms to focus on growing their competitiveness (Kotabe & Helsen, 2009; Peng, 2011; Zou, Kim & Cavusgil, 2009).

By and large, more welcoming domestic as well as global environments have facilitated firms from emerging nations to grow their exports and profits by ensuring that their products and work are appreciated by the global customer (Doole & Lowe, 2008; Zou & Fu, 2011). The environments enable the firms to stave off the challenges that are posed by the businesses that come to invest in the emerging economies. Sources indicate that institutions that are not friendly in advanced economies can limit the growth of exports by firms from developing economies. Clearly, institutions may constrain and enable global business, including exports (Solomon, Marshall & Stuart, 2008). Firms from emerging nations, which are exposed to global environments, may suffer from the pervasive consequence of generation of liabilities by the environments. Even then, the firms' adaptation to such environments has not been amply researched on in the past. The GBE literature and research have in the past been predominantly zeroed in on the modes of foreign entry, location resolutions, novel organizational type of models, partnerships, cultural variability, and the variables that are attendant to marketing (Freeman, Styles & Lawley, 2012; Kotabe & Helsen, 2009; Peng, 2011; Yi, Zhong & Zheng, 2012; Zou, Kim & Cavusgil, 2009). Every one of them incorporates a GBE component, in various instances, disparities in cultures, and in others measures that relate to the economy (Dekkers, 2009; Devinney, Pedersen & Tihanyi, 2010).

Regardless of the mounting efforts in researches within global business studies, much of the classical or traditional studies were driven by economists. They perceived the firms' advantages as shaped in exogenous ways (Solomon, Marshall & Stuart, 2008). It is only recently that the researchers shifted their attention towards appreciably managerial theories, and aspects. One of the most famous global business theories asserts that any firm will adjust to match the realities of the local business conditions. In such a case, adaptation will entail processes of acquiring knowledge as well as experiences, which allow and assist firms to evaluate opportunities and risks (Doole & Lowe, 2008; Zou & Fu, 2011). For example, the psychic distance, which is constituted by physical or geographic, economic, and cultural distances, shows the variations between each firm's host economy and home economy (Adis, 2010; Kotabe & Helsen, 2009; Lages, José & Cristiana, 2008; Peng, 2011; Sousa & Lengler, 2009; Zou, Kim & Cavusgil, 2009).

Firms globalize any of their operations or tasks first to adjacent economies. As they grow their experience, they certainly seek more faraway economies or markets, and dedicate more resources to them. The mode of entry strategy is thus always responsive to local realities, even as the firms expand in terms of their market reaches. This evidences a fractional acknowledgment of GBEs' complexity (Dess, Pinkham & Yang, 2011; Tantong, Karande, Nair & Singhapakdi, 2010; Solomon, Marshall & Stuart, 2008).

Current developments in the appraisal of the internationalization of firms have zeroed in on the costs that are exerted by or attendant to the environments that host them (Daub, 2009; Hoskisson & Hoskisson, 2008; Kaufmann & Roesch, 2012; Oshri, Kotlarsky & Willcocks, 2009; Zhou, Wu & Barnes, 2012). This is especially so if the host markets or economies are significantly dissimilar to the home markets and economies of the particular firms. The difference in the economies or markets is commonly christened as the 'foreignness liability'. Largely, the costs exploration is thought to have been initially persuaded by a 1960's seminal work by Hymer (Kotabe & Helsen, 2009; Peng, 2011; Zou, Kim & Cavusgil, 2009).

The concept that Hymer put forth focused on costs that are attendant to exports. This is an extensive concept that incorporates varied costs that emerge for exporting firms. In dealing with the liability, there is a need for adaptation to the host behaviors, norms as well as rules (Doole & Lowe, 2008; Zou & Fu, 2011). Although there is wide-ranging research that has been carried out in recent times, the researches concern themselves with the fundamental ideas, and regardless of the employed lenses, they are highly inclined towards treating their unsuccessful export performance or outcomes as emanating from unfitting choices relating to the selected entry mode, location, or the transactional models (Solomon, Marshall & Stuart, 2008).

Various works have presented the combination of the factors in the paradigm of Internalization-Location-Ownership (ILO) while others propose the Location-Ownership-Adjustment-Mode (LOMA). The LOMA proposal incorporates adaptation to GBEs as the principal dimension (Solomon, Marshall & Stuart, 2008). To appreciate what the adaptation should be, one should appreciate the GBE constituents beyond generic statements regarding external aspects or factors. Researchers require frameworks, which entail the GBE in its multi-dimensionality and complexity. However, much of the present researches seemingly employ the cultural typology that was postulated by Hofstede in establishing variations among different economies or countries (Doole & Lowe, 2008; Zou & Fu, 2011).

The typology continues to support researchers and businesss persons with comparable and quantitative cultural measures across economies or nations, consequently allowing theoretical as well as statistical comparisons. Nonetheless, such variations are more extensive than being merely cultural (Dekkers, 2009; Devinney, Pedersen & Tihanyi, 2010). Thus, GBE constructs should take views that integrate many of the environment-related variables. The broader, multi-dimensional, and more sophisticated GBE renders the direction of exporting, and other global operations, separate from domestic businesses or firms that operate on a large scale (Ahmed & Rock, 2012; He & Wei, 2011). In adapting to the GBE, exporting firms need methodical gathering of data on every environment-relate dimension as well as any economic-type agents within the local economies or markets (Doole & Lowe, 2008; Zou & Fu, 2011).

The data should be processed and employed to enhance knowledge regarding the export environments, operations, and realities. Then, the firms should make out their internal operations or areas that are vulnerable as well as external openings towards more effectual fit in the host environment, in addition to the domestic environment (Kotabe & Helsen, 2009; Peng, 2011; Zou, Kim & Cavusgil, 2009). Lastly, the firms should be keen to actualize best practices that are well modified, adjusted, and adapted to the environments that are identified. Any of the firm's capability for adapting to such environments is largely presented as a resource. The resource's foundation is firmly within the experience and knowledge stock of human resources that are aimed at better fits in heightening their export performance (Ahmed & Rock, 2012; He & Wei, 2011). Several sources assert that it is additionally crucial in firming the firms' competitive advantages within the highly competitive GBE and export circles (Dekkers, 2009; Devinney, Pedersen & Tihanyi, 2010). The competition faced by the firms does not acquire neoclassical equilibriums in the long-term (Solomon, Marshall & Stuart, 2008).

The linkages between global adaptation strategies as well as export performances of varied firms are subject to and, dependent on the accumulated globalization experience. The relation, as it concerns new global firms, is U-shaped, while that of experienced global firms is positive (Kotabe & Helsen, 2009; Peng, 2011; Zou, Kim & Cavusgil, 2009). The process of adaptation hinges on learning though it is not essentially characterized as such. Consistent and sustainable capability for adaptation draws benefits from the grasp of the process, especially in relation to environmental type of diversity. In reality, it is not mandatory that competitive advantages are based on multiple resources. The ability of firms from emerging economies to adapt is probably buttressed by skills in commercial, financial, technological, marketing, and technical, or other fields, or employees' or firms' entrepreneurial competencies (Solomon, Marshall & Stuart, 2008). The learning is seen as being capable of giving off competitive advantages to exporting firms. In actuality, it is not the learning that occasions the varied advantages (Doole & Lowe, 2008; Zou & Fu, 2011). The advantages stream from any resources that are deployed. The mastery of learning by a firm may not give rise to enhanced fiscal or export performance. Adaptation is premised on the exporting firm's survival and performance core (Dekkers, 2009; Devinney, Pedersen & Tihanyi, 2010).

Some exporters learn via competition and through their comparative export performance, matched against that of their competitors, and their positioning of resources, and consequently their own relative advantages as well as disadvantages (Dekkers, 2009; Devinney, Pedersen & Tihanyi, 2010). Some meta-national firms harness the intellectual abilities and resources from across the nations where they have set exporting bases (Kotabe & Helsen, 2009; Peng, 2011; Zou, Kim & Cavusgil, 2009). They integrate the abilities and resources in ways that effectually advance their strategic aims and export targets in the long-term. Such meta-nationals have odd adaptation capacities. The global adaptation strategies for exporting firms from emerging economies are endogenous (Doole & Lowe, 2008; Zou & Fu, 2011). They grow from being focused on internal competitiveness to being externally, and legitimately external. Adaptation is clearly considered in many sources as being a resource that is strategic (Solomon, Marshall & Stuart, 2008). The extant literature does not demonstrate that an exporting firm's global adaptation strategies change if they grow into meta-nationals. No research has been carried to conclusively determine whether the extent of a firm's adaptation affects its export performance. Generally, much of the extant literature acknowledges that exporting firms should adapt to the GBE. To explain further on the idea of standardization/adaption of exporting firms, the following section addresses the two strategies separately.

Standardization

Standardization of international marketing strategy is concerned about "using a common product, price, distribution, and promotion program on a worldwide basis" (Jain, 1989, p. 70). Standardization includes two aspects: 1) marketing program; and 2) marketing process. While marketing program pertains to the marketing mix variables, marketing process relates to the tools that help firms to develop and implement marketing program (Jain, 1989). Adaptation and standardization are two concepts of the same continuum (Shoham, 1996). In other words, the higher the degree of standardization of the marketing mix, the lower the degree of adaptation of the marketing mix is (Cavusgil, Zou & Naidu, 1993).

Levitt (1983) posits that the wishes and demands of the people around the globe are getting more and more homogenous. Differences in tastes and practices among people will soon vanish. Whereas global company operates around the world as a single market achieving economies of scale, multinational corporations do their business in different countries by customizing and adapting their products and activities, and subjecting themselves to high costs. He argues that effective global companies, striving for global convergence, achieve economies of scale by targeting the world as if it were composed of several standardized markets. Because of the high volume scale from modern production facilities, it is more economical to serve one or two separate markets with standardized products. Global companies adapt "reluctantly" their products to the local differences or wishes. Technology and globalization create a more similar globe and lead to economies- of-scale. Global firms of low prices, high quality, and reliability are capable of producing standardized products all over the world because diversity will converge, resulting in lower costs and prices.

Douglas and Craig (1986) assume that there are many benefits related to standardization: (1) economies-of-scale in production and marketing; (2) transfer of know-how or experience; (3) uniform image; and (4) easier control and coordination.

Barker and Ay din (1991) believe that: (1) economies of scale in R&D, marketing, and production; and (2) easier market entry and operation, are the two main factors of standardization of the marketing mix. These benefits which are related to standardization depend upon the belief that world markets are converging in terms of tastes, preferences, standards of living, and legal environment.

Shoham (1995, 1996a, 1996b, 1999, 2002) assumes that economies of scale and the desire to present consistent and high quality image across local boundaries are the main factors for standardization of the marketing program. We can attain economies-of- scale in the areas of production, logistics, distribution, research and development, advertising and promotion, and targeting inter-market cross country segments. Global firms can deliver high quality products and programs by concentrating on research and development and management of the total value chain.

To summarize, standardization of international marketing strategy is related to the employment of a common price, product, promotion, and distribution strategy across international markets. The main motivators of standardization are believed to be economies-of-scale, delivery of consistent image and product, easier control and coordination of the marketing program, and easier market entry and penetration.

Adaptation

Adaptation of international marketing strategy relates to "using tailor-made product, price, distribution, and promotion programs for each market" (Shoham, 1996a, p. 6). Adaptation, in the international marketing literature, is related to two concepts: (1) marketing program; and (2) marketing process. Whereas marketing program is related to the marketing mix variables, marketing process relates to the means that help firms to develop and implement marketing program (Jain, 1989).

Hill and Still (1984) suggest that the extent of standardization (or adaptation) is influenced by multinational and international product polices, in addition to cultural and economic differences. The authors, in an empirical study of multinational corporations, found out that product adaptation is essential either because of environmental conditions such as legal, climatic, and economic issues or local competition. To increase the international firms' market position in each local market due to local custom and culture, Hill and Still recommend an adaptation strategy of marketing program for international firms.

Boddewyn, Soehl, and Picard (1986) state that there are still three main hindrances to standardization: (1) national differences in tastes, habits, regulation, and technical requirements; (2) competition; and (3) economic condition of the target market.

Kotler (1986) believes that there are three major motivators for adaptation in foreign markets: (1) degree of variations of customer requirements for special product features across countries; (2) differences in customers' buying behavior and their resources across international markets; and (3) variation of environmental conditions, such as governmental rules, climate, and competition in international markets. Being conscious of the different food regulations and laws across foreign markets, products such as Coca-Cola and McDonald's adopt a "Plan global, act local" approach.

Wind (1986) suggests the "think globally, act locally" approach to develop a global marketing strategy. He stresses that a global marketing strategy has a global consideration of the competitive and dynamic market conditions and considers the uniqueness of each country.

Total uniformity or standardization, as registered by Walters (1986), is a very unique case in marketing programs. Adapting international marketing programs are necessary for many reasons: (1) difference in the firm's strategic situation in each local market; (2) benefits which are achieved from standardization might be unexpected due to the lack of hard data; and (3) absence of evidence of more rapid diffusion of products and ideas across national boundaries. Cultural and environmental differences have also prohibited the use of a total uniform approach in international marketing programs. Marketing programs are influenced by the differences in legal environment and local idiosyncrasies, thus leading to adaptation strategy.

Because of the absence of evidence of homogenization of global markets, as emphasized by Douglas and Wind (1987), and flexible factory automation, a standardized marketing strategy is not suitable when applying a global marketing strategy. Douglas and Craig (1986) argue that there are obstacles to standardization; these obstacles include governmental rules, differences in customer wishes, nature of the marketing infrastructure, the nature of the competitive structure in foreign markets and responses nature.

Therefore, the authors identify three global strategy concepts: (1) pure standardization; (2) pure differentiation; and (3) hybrid strategy. Companies should utilize a hybrid strategy as opposed to a very limited one by adopting a global and universal perspective of developing marketing strategies and deciding opportunities across national boundaries to achieve scale economies and potential synergies, and use a pure differentiation strategy to adapt to different customer wishes and tastes in different countries.

Barker and Aydin (1991) claim that standardization of marketing strategies across national boundaries cannot be performed without taking into consideration environmental factors, such as product, industry characteristics, infrastructure, and consumers' desires and buying patterns. For example, Coca-Cola, a highly globalized company, adapts soft drinks to local tastes and preferences with respect to size, ingredient, and type of containers. Moreover, the income levels throughout the world are changeable. As a result, such difference prevents consumers from less-developed countries purchasing global products. Lastly, governmental rules in each country are changeable, especially in sectors such as health, safety, and environment. The argument that local differences in tastes and preferences are cultural and that a firm not employing a standardization or globalization strategy is destined to fail can be very misleading.

Despite the fact that benefits such as cost savings, qualified planning, and control are obtained from standardization, Barker (1993) notes that firms that utilize a standardized strategy without any change and improvement will have difficulties in sustaining growth and profitability, arising from competitors' adaptation or differentiation strategies. Cultural, social, and environmental factors are mandatory elements that force companies to modify and adapt elements of the marketing mix.

Positioning, theory of friction, and strategic flexibility, as noted by Shoham (1995, 1996a, 1996b, 1999, 2002), are the three main motivators for adaptation of marketing program. Price difference happens when the level of homogeneity across countries is lower than that of within borders. Firms can offset the lower costs associated with economies-of-scale by deciding a higher price through accurate positioning and adaptation in a given market, thus increasing sales and profits. There are costs not only incurred from economies-of-scale, but also those that arise from the friction between headquarters and local subsidiaries. Theory of friction is associated with the hidden costs when friction occurs between the home and host market organizations because of cultural differences, government regulations, marketing institutions, and physical environment. Strategic flexibility helps firms to communicate quickly and flexibly to the changing need of the local market environment, as the Japanese firms did in the past.

Yip (2003, p. 141) notes that "global marketing is not about standardizing the marketing process". The components of marketing mix, such as product design, product and brand positioning, advertising, promotion, and distribution, should be more flexible and global in contrast to others. Global marketing strategy does not need to be 100 per cent uniform in content or coverage. Rather, "It is not a blind adherence to standardization of all marketing elements" (p. 141).

To summarize, the decision of export firms, whether to adapt or standardize their products and strategies, depends largely on how the firm predicts that choice will benefit their objectives and performance. The best theories that explain the constructs of adaptation and standardization, particularly in emerging countries' context, are the contingency theory and the strategic fit approach that originate from the contingency theory (Park, 2006). The following section addresses the contingency theory and strategic fit approach in export firms.

Contingency Approach

Contingency theory is a class of behavioral theory that claims that there is no best way to organize a corporation, to lead a company, or to make decisions. Instead, the optimal course of action is contingent (dependent) upon the internal and external situation. Several contingency approaches were developed concurrently in the late 1960s. They suggested that previous theories such as Weber's bureaucracy and Taylor's scientific management had failed because they neglected that management style and organizational structure were influenced by various aspects of the environment: the contingency factors. There could not be "one best way" for leadership or organization. Historically, contingency theory has sought to formulate broad generalizations about the formal structures that are typically associated with or best fit the use of different technologies. The perspective originated with the work of Joan Woodward (1958), who argued that technologies directly determine differences in such organizational attributes as span of control, centralization of authority, and the formalization of rules and procedures.

The ongoing debate regarding standardization versus adaptation has driven scholars to shift to another view known as the contingency perspective; a perspective basically derived from the contingency theory where the basic principle is that the best practices depend on the contingencies of the situation. Researchers have accepted the fact that neither a wholly implemented standardization nor adaptation of marketing program is effective in the international markets. According to the contingency perspective, standardization/adaption decision is a process comprising a number of antecedent factors (Akaah, 1991; Jain, 1989; Rau & Preble, 1987). Contingency theorists claim that corporate performance greatly depends on the successful alignment, or referred to as the strategic fit between an organization's internal processes that includes strategy, structure, and resources, and the external environment (Burns & Stalker, 1967; Aldrich, 1979; Keats & Hitt, 1988).

This particular view states that neither standardization nor adaptation can be viewed in an isolated situation and both should be considered as the two ends forming the same continuum, upon which the level of firms' marketing strategy standardization/adaptation move between them (Cavusgil, Zou & Naidu, 1993; Theodisou & Leonidou, 2003). The decision of the firm to either standardize or adapt based on this view, is specific to a situation after a thorough analysis and assessment of all the crucial contingency factors existing in a specific market at a specific time. In addition, according to the contingency perspective, the suitability of the chosen level of the degree of standardization/ adaptation should be determined based on its effect on a company's export performance in the international markets (Quelch & Hoff, 1986; Jain, 1989; Onkvist & Shaw, 1990; Cavusgil & Zou, 1994). Consequently, the challenge faced by the international firm is to identify which of the strategic elements are suitable, in which environment and up to which level.

Rau and Preble (1987) stress that despite the different perspectives taken by the researchers according to the level of standardization attainable, there has been a consensus of level of standardization that can be achieved. It is possible for firms to determine the degree of standardization based on the following: similarity of markets and internal organizational costs, mode of entry, such as fully-owned versus joint venture, and brand name, such as international versus local, stage in product life cycle and breadth of product line, and size of the market and level of inter-penetration. Jain (1989) claims that the level of standardization of marketing program is dependent upon different factors, like target market which comprises geographic area and economic factors; market position which comprises similarity between the home and local market, consumer behavior and lifestyles, cultural distance; and a firm's competitive position which comprises market leader position, nature of product like industrial versus consumer durable products, environmental factors like weather and size of homes in different areas, legal like law and regulation, and political environment, marketing infrastructure such as retailers, wholesalers, warehousing, transportation, etc., and organization including corporate orientation, headquarters-subsidiary relationship and delegation of authority factors.

Akaah (1991) revealed that consumer characteristics, behavior, nature of ownership, such as some ownership interest versus no ownership interest, and corporate orientation, such as ethnocentric/polycentric versus egiocentric or geocentric, significantly relate to the level of standardization, particularly when there exists a similarity in consumer characteristics and behavior between the home and host nation. Also, in cases where firms have ownership interest in host country business, they utilize a greater level of standardization of marketing program. However, firms displaying ethnocentric orientation exhibit a higher degree of standardization of the marketing program as opposed to those displaying geocentric orientation. Generally speaking, this approach considers both standardization and adaptation as the two sides of the same continuum in which their degree is based on a number of antecedent factors.

Strategic Fit Perspective

This perspective stems from the contingency perspective because the scholars have failed to comprehend the configuration of the firm's antecedent factors. In addition, it has been generally believed that an important notion within the strategic management and marketing strategy paradigm is the alignment of the organization's internal and external factors (antecedent factors) with the firm's strategy (Galbraith & Kazanjian, 1986). The proponents of the contingency theory claim that performance results increase when there exists an alignment or 'fit' between a firm's external environment, its internal factors and its strategy (Burns & Stalker, 1967; Lawrence & Lorsch, 1967; Keats & Hitt, 1988).

Strategic fit represents the level to which an organization matches its resources and capabilities with the opportunities existing in the external environment. This matching normally happens through the strategy and thus, it is necessary that the company owns actual resources and capabilities so as to carry out and support the selected strategy. According to Nadler and Tushman (1979), the greater the aggregate level of congruence or fit between the different components, the greater the effectiveness of the organization. This, will in turn, result in higher degrees of goal achievement, resources usage, and adaptation. Various previous strategic fit models differed on the basis of the contingent factors considered and the type of strategic analysis. Basically, the 'fit' principle takes into consideration the level of alignment existing between competitive situation, strategy, organizational culture and leadership style. In this essence, alignment is considered as the 'suitability' of the different elements with one another.

The view regarding strategic alignment's emanation from strategic management and organization theory research has it fundamental base on the notion that organizational performance is a result of consistency or "fit" between two or more factors, such as structure, strategy, and technology (Burns and Stalker, 1967). In the above perspective, coherence is an active search that seeks to match the organization with the environment it is running in and to organize the resources in order to support this match (Miles and Snow, 1984, p. 11). Because strategy is the mediating force between the firm and its environment, it is a general alignment technique that is specifically compatible with the organization's technology that is pivotal in creating significant competitive advantage.

Several researches carried out in the US, Europe and Australia reveal that excellent performance determined in different ways are linked with high levels of alignment between four elements, i.e., competitive situation, strategy, organizational culture and leadership style, and the extent to which the activities in the organization complement each other in a way that leads to competitive advantage (Galbraith & Kazanjian, 1986; Venkatraman & Prescott, 1990; Chorn, 1991; Habib & Victor, 1991; Naman & Slevin, 1993; Stimpert & Duhaime, 1997). The advantages of good fit comprise cost reduction, resulting from economies-of-scale, and the transfer of knowledge and skills.

The basic idea of environment-strategy co-alignment influences contingency theory work in international marketing. Previous studies targeted relationships between internationally active firm's market environment, its marketing strategy and its performance on the basis of the structure-conduct-performance framework of industrial organization (IO) economics (Cavusgil and Zou 1994; Özsomer and Simonin, 2004; Sousa and Bradley, 2008). The aim of the above mentioned work is to pinpoint the full and partial mediation patterns that are present among the constructs, like a larger collection of environmental and organizational factors, which are conducive to firms' adaptation that assist in firm's performance (Calantone *et al.* 2006). Nevertheless, descriptive contingency theory researches do not normally hope to get a response to observed inconsistency in the adaptation-performance relationship (Shoham, 2002).

There exists many ways of modeling the influence of fit between environment and strategy on performance (Venkatraman, 1989). The superior way in international marketing research has been "fit as moderation," with environmental variables conditioning the adaptation-performance relationship. However, the moderation perspective has not been displayed by the data in some researches (Shoham 1999; Xu, Cavusgil, and White, 2006), and therefore, Xu, Cavusgil, and White (2006) were led to call for more theoretical justification in future applications of contingency theory in international marketing strategy research. Aligned with a systems theory approach to contingency theory, environment-product strategy fit to export performance relationships can only develop by simultaneously considering the different contingencies existing around complex organizations (Katsikeas, Samiee & Theodosiou, 2006; Calantone *et al.*, 2006). International marketers generally work in multiple and mostly conflicting contingencies (Govindarajan, 1988; Griffith, 2011). Owing to this reason, the systems approach may be considered as a reaction to the potential reductionism of fit as moderation (Drazin and Van de Ven, 1985; Tan and Litschert, 1994). Contrarily, using fit as matching, Katsikeas, Samiee, and Theodosiou (2006) reveal the external environment marketing strategy standardization co-alignment is positively related to performance.

Katsikeas, Samiee, and Theodosiou (2006); Xu, Cavusgil, and White (2006) consider contingency theory as the explanation to the product adaptation-performance relationship. The authors claim that there exists no universal strategic option for adaptation which is optimal for all firms and circumstances and which would also explain the ambiguity in the findings of the few studies on exporting that have looked into the performance implications of product adaptation. Their argument is compounded by the notion that product adaptation is not normally linked to export performance.

Current international marketing strategy and contingency theory researches (Albaum and Tse 2001; Özsomer & Simonin 2004; Sousa and Bradley, 2008) have concentrated on studying environment structure → strategy conduct → performance associations. There some empirical researches (e.g., Katsikeas, Samiee, and Theodosiou, 2006; Xu, Cavusgil, and White, 2006) that employed the normative model of contingency theory to international marketing strategy adaptation/standardization. Fit as alignment has performance relevance as opposed to the inconclusive findings revealed in previous studies using moderation as a form of fit (Shoham, 1999). The finding that adaptation is an influential variable, even if it is not directly related to performance, is specifically worth keeping in mind.

Prior studies concerning exporting have almost always holistically considered marketing-mix elements and utilized global or higher order reflective conceptualizations possessing single path coefficient to performance (Katsikeas, Samiee, and Theodosiou 2006; Özsomer and Simonin, 2004). But several prior researches (Cavusgil and Zou 1994; Lages, Jap, and Griffith, 2008) have revealed performance relevance of adaptation differing throughout the components of the marketing program. This study posits that it is timely and meaningful to look into specific dimensions of the marketing mix. The studies which tackled individual marketing-mix elements have isolated promotion as the key adaptation/standardization concern (Jain, 1989; Özsomer and Simonin, 2004). This study contributes to the body of work by focusing on the marketing mix decision, which is at the vanguard of exporters' marketing strategy decision making (Theodosiou & Leonidou, 2003).

EXPORT MARKETING STRATEGY

Export marketing strategy can be defined as the "means by which a firm responds to the interplay of internal and external forces to meet the objectives of the export venture" (Cavusgil & Zou, 1994, p. 4).

The components of which an export marketing strategy is established, have been mixed across the literature. Cavusgil and Kirpalani (1993) observe that export marketing strategy includes product, promotion, distribution, and marketing capability. Export marketing strategy is related to the traditional marketing plan, such as pricing, promotion, distribution, and product (Cavusgil & Zou, 1994). However, Cooper and Kleinschmidt (1985) point out that export marketing strategy refers to the product adaptation policy and market selection. De Luz (1993) notes that an export strategy consists of quality control, management motivation, international business training, marketing research, target nations, competitive pricing, standardization of product, and direct distribution. In addition, Koh and Robicheaux (1988) observe that export marketing variables are product modification; export pricing compared to the US market, currency, dealer, brand name, and channel strategies. Stewart and McAuley (2000) point out that export marketing strategy consists of five aspects: (1) market scope; (2) the degree of product adaptation; (3) the degree of promotional adaptation; 4) the level of support given to the foreign distribution channel; and 5) pricing strategy.

Aaby and Slater (1989), who examined 55 empirical studies in the field of export literature from 1978 to 1988, state that export marketing strategy includes market selection, product, pricing, promotion, and distribution strategy. Chetty and Hamilton (1993) conclude that export marketing strategy includes market selection, use of intermediaries, product mix, product development, promotion, pricing, and staffing according to a review of 111 empirical studies in the export literature between 1978 and 1991. Zou and Stan (1998), who depend upon the review of 50 empirical studies in export literature from 1987 to 1997, show that product adaptation, product strength, promotion adaptation, promotion intensity, price adaptation, competitive pricing, channel relationships, and type of channels form an export marketing strategy.

In short, export marketing strategy is a tool used by firms to respond to the internal and external factors and to achieve their aims in the export venture. The literature emphasizes that marketing mix components seem to be a crucial part of the export marketing strategy. This study does not tackle market selection, whether industrialized or less developed countries are chosen.

Therefore, the focus of this research is the adaptation/standardization of the marketing mix of the export marketing strategy.

DETERMINANTS OF THE DEGREE OF ADAPTATION OF EXPORT MARKETING STRATEGY

As discussed before, the contingency perspective (Jain, 1989) considers both standardization and adaptation as two faces of the same coin and decides the degree of standardization (or adaptation) depending on internal and external forces. Since then, researchers have expanded Jain's (1989) contingency framework to develop a model that is suitable in the export context.

Depending on the previous studies on strategic framework, Cavusgil and Zou (1994) claim that export marketing strategy (i.e., the extent of standardization) is decided by internal (e.g., firm and product factors) and external (e.g., industry and export market characteristics) factors. Firm characteristics include international knowledge, extent of international business involvement, and resource obtainable for export development. Product factors include culture-specificity of product (i.e., culture-specific products have to be appropriate to the culture of the export market), product uniqueness, firm's experience with product, and product's technical complexity. Industry factors refer to technology forcefulness, and intensity of price competition. Export market characteristics include export market attractiveness, cultural/legal similarity of markets, export market competitive intensity, and knowledge of export customers.

Cavusgil, Zou, and Naidu (1993), expanding the previous framework of Jain (1989), claim that the degree of the adaptation of the export marketing strategy is a function of product characteristics (product uniqueness, cultural specificity of product, kind of product), industry characteristics (technology orientation of industry), firm characteristics (international experience, export sales goal for the venture, entry scope), and export market characteristics (similarity of legal regulations, export market competitiveness, and product familiarity of export customers).

Environmental conditions, as suggested by Shoham (1999), influence export managers to decide the extent of standardization (adaptation) in export ventures. He observes that seven environmental conditions, as derived from the work of Jain (1989), are most likely to influence the degree of standardization: (1) exporting country image; (2) competitive position (e.g., market share); (3) competition structure (e.g., existence of similar competitors); (4) differences in local law; (5) local government influence; (6) physical climate (e.g., climate, building density, and building size);and (7) marketing infrastructure (e.g., distribution infrastructure, media infrastructure).

Chung (2002) creates a framework in the light of Jain's study (1989) that depicts the relationship between internal and external factors that influence the degree of adaptation strategy. Chung notes that the degree of adaptation strategy is a function of firm factors, target country factors, and product factors. Firm factors consist of international experience, market entry mode (i.e., high resource commitment entry mode versus low resource commitment entry mode), and immigrant effect (i.e., firms controlled or established by immigrants). Target country factors include government regulations, economic development, and marketing environment. Product factors include kind of product and product life cycle.

Depending on the review of previous studies of Jain (1989), Cavusgil and Zou (1994), Cavusgil, Zou, and Naidu (1993), Chung (2002), and Shoham (1999), decide the variables that affect the extent of standardization can be classified into firm factors, product factors, industry factors, and export market characteristics.

In the current research and building on the discussions and arguments above, a number of antecedent factors are hypothesized to influence the marketing mix and in turn the export performance of the Malaysian companies. These factors include international experience, technology intensity, competition level, government regulation, cultural differences, economic differences, country image, physical condition, and marketing infrastructure. Furthermore, the framework designed for the present research is grounded on the way these factors affect the marketing mix in the Malaysian export companies. Then, the way marketing mix influences the export performance is examined. The components of the framework are discussed in further detail and the relevant research hypotheses are presented in the following section.

KEY DETERMINANTS AND RESEARCH HYPOTHESIS

International Experience

The concept of international experience is related to the level of experience accumulated the firm as an international business player (Cavusgil & Zou, 1994). International experience allows firms to account for dissimilarities between markets and react to the idiosyncrasies of each local market with a modified marketing strategy (Terpstra, 1987).

Douglas and Craig (1989) posit that as firms get international experience, marketing strategy, such as advertising, sales promotion, product, pricing, and distribution strategies should be adapted to the local market conditions in order to get along with the market more quickly. A qualified firm that is conscious of the differences in foreign business environment and market conditions is more likely to adopt a modified marketing strategy (Cavusgil,

Zou & Naidu, 1993; Hill & Still, 1984). By contrast, less qualified and experienced firms endeavor to correspond between their product offerings and local market conditions so that the extent of adaptation of the marketing program can be minimized, thus reducing operational risks (Douglas & Craig, 1989). Inexperienced firms in direct marketing also meet difficulties in deciding the extent of adaptation and tailoring their marketing strategy to meet the local market conditions (Robles & Akhter, 1997).

In an analytical study of US exporters, Cavusgil, Zou, and Naidu (1993) state that international experience is positive in terms of the extent of adaptation of product and promotion strategy. In a similar vein, Cavusgil and Zou (1994) believe that the extent of product adaptation is positively affected by the amount of international experience of the firm.

An example about this would be in the case of some early Korean exporters; in the early 1980s, with little international business experience, they mostly depended on original equipment manufacturer (OEM) to present products in foreign markets, thus reducing operational risk. For example, Eunsung Corporation, a manufacturer of fishing poles, mainly depended on OEM when first entering the US market. However, when they became more internationally experienced and qualified, they began to use their own brand 'Silstar', and utilized a more localized strategy by introducing fashionable fishing poles to meet the local market conditions and to increase their market presence. Consequently, the company earned market share of 40 per cent in the US fishing pole market (Kim, 2004). Another example in the Korean context is AMOREPACIFIC, a leading Korean cosmetics company, which faced difficulties when it first entered the French market, since it presented the 'Soon' brand without major modifications to its marketing strategy. In effect, it showed a bad performance, leaving its product covered with a cloud of dust on the store shelves (Chang, 2004).

Firms, which are more adept in international experience, are more likely to adopt an adapted marketing strategy in foreign markets to meet the specialty of each local market. That is to say, the more international experience the firm gets, the degree of adaptation of the marketing mix increases. Based on the previous discussion, the following hypotheses are introduced:

> *Hypothesis 1:* The greater the international experience, the greater the likelihood that Malaysian exporters will adapt their marketing mix strategy.
> *H1a:* The greater the international experience, the greater the likelihood that Malaysian exporters will adapt their product strategy.
> *H1b:* The greater the international experience, the greater the likelihood that Malaysian exporters will adapt their promotion strategy.

H1c: The greater the international experience, the greater the likelihood that Malaysian exporters will adapt their distribution strategy.

H1d: The greater the international experience, the greater the likelihood that Malaysian exporters will adapt their pricing strategy.

Technology Intensity

Standardized marketing strategy is more suitable for technology-intensive products, such as computer hardware, aircrafts, semiconductors, photographic equipment, heavy equipment, and machine tools than less technology- intensive or traditional products, such as clothing, food, toiletries, and household cleaners, because the latter product category is more sensitive and appeals to tastes, customs, and habits of each society (Cavusgil & Zou, 1994; Cavusgil, Zou & Naidu, 1993; Levitt, 1983). In short, if a product meets universal needs of customers, it requires less adaptation (Jain, 1989). For instance, Corning ware's "oven-to-freezer" feature was very popular in the US, while it did not carve out a big market share in France. Rather, a soufflé dish was more popular than "oven to freezer" in France. Corning Glass Works, on the other hand, introduced its electronic and medical products with a standardized marketing strategy because it regarded its product as universal product that did not differ much across international markets (Jain, 1989).

Cavusgil and Zou (1994) observe that firms participating in technology intensive industries should employ a competitive (adapted) pricing strategy to widen their demand base in export markets because it is important to recover the initial large investments in modern technology.

In accordance with the previous discussion, the following hypotheses are made:

Hypothesis 2: The greater the technology intensity, the greater the likelihood that Malaysian exporters will adapt their marketing mix strategy.

H2a: Technology intensity of the industry is positively associated with the degree of product adaptation of Malaysian exporters.

H2b: Technology intensity is negatively associated with the degree of promotion adaptation of Malaysian exporters.

H2c: Technology intensity is negatively associated with the degree of distribution adaptation of Malaysian exporters.

H2d. Technology intensity is positively associated with the degree of price adaptation of Malaysian exporters.

Competition Level

In the presence of international competition in export markets, an organization needs to modify its marketing strategy. This is done in an attempt to meet the tastes and desires of customers in foreign markets to gain a competitive position over its rivals (Cavusgil, Zou & Naidu, 1993; Hill & Still, 1984; Jain, 1989), leading to local market expansion and entry to new market segments (Douglas & Craig, 1989). On the contrary, in the absence of competition, an organization may continuously perform well in foreign markets with a standardized marketing strategy (Jain, 1989). Jain's (1989) main argument is that standardized marketing strategy is more suitable under less competition.

Peebles and Ryans (1984) argue that promotional practices and promotion budget may need to be modified across foreign markets to meet competitor's offerings and promotion expenditures, and to assault their promotional messages. Furthermore, Czinkota and Ronkainen (1990) note that a firm's distribution strategy should be matched to the effectiveness and productivity of rival's distribution channels. This is to facilitate not losing its competitive position in foreign markets.

Furthermore, in an empirical study of US exporters, Cavusgil *et al.* (1993) found that the degree of adaptation of promotion strategy was positively related to the level of competition. Cavusgil and Zou (1994) also found that the degree of adaptation of product and promotion strategy was positively affected by the level of competition in an empirical study of US exporters.

The studies reviewed above seem to suggest that the higher the intensity of competition in international markets, the greater the need to adapt the marketing strategy. Furthermore, an adapted marketing strategy allows firms to match the idiosyncrasies of customers in international markets and ultimately gain a competitive position over the local competition.

Based upon the preceding discussion, it can also be anticipated that Malaysian exporters will follow the same argument that as the intensity of competition increases in foreign markets, exporters will adapt their marketing strategy.

In accordance with the previous discussion, the following hypotheses are made:

> *Hypothesis 3:* The greater the competition level of the industry, the greater the likelihood that Malaysian exporters will adapt their marketing mix strategy.
>
> *H3a:* The competition level of the industry is related to the degree of product adaptation of Malaysian exporters.
>
> *H3b:* The competition level of the industry is related to the degree of promotion adaptation of Malaysian exporters.

H3c: The competition level of the industry is related to the degree of distribution adaptation of Malaysian exporters.
H3d: The competition level of the industry is related to the degree of price adaptation of Malaysian exporters.

Government Regulations

Governmental rules such as product standards, patents, tariffs, non-tariffs, and state participation in business affect all trends of the marketing program, thus necessitating an adaptation of marketing program in international markets (Jain, 1989). Buzzell (1968) observes that differences in legal rules between the home and host market confine the standardization of marketing strategy. Legal restrictions in host countries aim at protecting the citizens of host countries to guarantee the safety of foreign products (Johnson & Arunthanes, 1995).

In an empirical study of US exporters, Cavusgil *et al.* (1993) found that the extent of product adaptation was negatively associated with the similarity of legal regulations between the home and host market. As similarity of governmental rules between home and host market increased, the extent of product adaptation decreased.

Governmental rules are normally an external element that is unmanageable by exporting countries and firms. For example, Lotte, a confectionary company, had to write down the product content information on the labeling in Chinese in response to governmental instructions (Park, 2006). Hyundai Motors, a Korean manufacturer, also had to supply cars with speed limit tools when it exported automobiles to the Middle East countries. Furthermore, the company had to equip cars with air bags to export to the North American market, where it is mandated by governmental rules (Park, 2006).

Depending upon the previous discussion, the following research hypotheses are generated:

Hypothesis 4: The greater the difference of government regulations, the greater the likelihood that Malaysian exporters will adapt their marketing mix strategy.
H4a: The greater the difference of government regulations between home and export market, the greater the likelihood that Malaysian exporters will adapt their product strategy.
H4b: The greater the difference of government regulations between home and export market, the greater the likelihood that Malaysian exporters will adapt their promotion strategy.
H4c: The greater the difference of government regulations between home and export market, the greater the likelihood that Malaysian exporters will adapt their distribution strategy.

H4d: The greater the difference of government regulations between home and export market, the greater the likelihood that Malaysian exporters will adapt their pricing strategy.

Cultural Differences

Culture is defined as the "entire heritage of a society transmitted by word or any other form and includes all traditions, habits, religion, art, and language" (Jeannett & Hennessey, 2001, p. 78). At the international level, it is important for marketers to understand culture that affects buyer behavior in foreign markets, which will ultimately formulate the nature of the international marketing policy (Jeannet & Hennessey, 2001). Consequently, cultural match between home and foreign markets necessitates the use of a standardized marketing policy (Jain, 1989).

To summarize, culture of each local market influences every aspect of the marketing policy. It can be assumed that cultural differences among international markets influence the degree of marketing program adaptation in foreign markets. One can also assume that Malaysian exporters will adopt the same position that cultural differences force them to modify their marketing policy.

Depending upon the previous discussion, the following research hypotheses are created:

Hypothesis 5: The greater the cultural differences between Malaysia and export market, the greater the likelihood that Malaysian exporters will adapt their marketing mix strategy.
H5a: The greater the cultural differences between Malaysia and export market, the greater the degree of product strategy adaptation of Malaysian exporters.
H5b: The greater the cultural differences between Malaysia and export market, the greater the degree of promotion strategy adaptation of Malaysian exporters.
H5c: The greater the cultural differences between Malaysia and export market, the greater the degree of distribution strategy adaptation of Malaysian exporters.
H5d: The greater the cultural differences between Malaysia and export market, the greater the degree of pricing strategy adaptation of Malaysian exporters.

Economic Differences

Buzzell (1968) posits that differences in the stage of economic and industrial development between national and international markets can have a vital influence on the choice of marketing policy. Jain's (1989) contingency framework suggests that a standardized marketing strategy is preferable among Organization for Economic Cooperation and Development (OECD) countries where the stage of economic development is similar.

Japanese firms, in the early 1980s, exported low-price and quality consumer electronics, motorcycles, and automobiles (compared to those introduced in Western Europe and the US) to Southeast Asia and Latin America where purchasing power was low (Jatusripitak, Fahey & Kotler, 1985).

To summarize, differences in the stage of economic development between national and international market affect the extent of marketing strategy adaptation of firms. The greater difference of economic development across foreign markets is likely to expand the extent of adaptation of the marketing policy. One can also expect that Malaysian exporters will adopt the same view that economic differences will force them to modify their marketing policy.

Depending upon the previous discussion, the following research hypotheses are made:

> *Hypothesis 6:* The greater the economic difference between the exporters' home market and foreign markets, the greater the likelihood that Malaysian exporters will adapt their marketing mix strategy.
> *H6a:* The greater the economic difference between the exporters' home market and foreign market, the greater the level of adaptation of product strategy of Malaysian exporters.
> *H6b:* The greater the economic difference between the exporters' home market and foreign market, the greater the level of adaptation of promotion strategy of Malaysian exporters.
> *H6c:* The greater the economic difference between the exporters' home market and foreign market, the greater the level of adaptation of distribution strategy of Malaysian exporters.
> *H6d:* The greater the economic difference between the exporters' home market and foreign market, the greater the level of adaptation of pricing strategy of Malaysian exporters.

Exporting Country Image

Country of origin effects is related to the "extent to which the place of manufacture influences product evaluations" (Albaum, Strandskov & Duerr, 2002, p. 408). Country of origin influences customer's perception and evaluation of a product (Baalbaki & Malhotra, 1993). Therefore, the country of origin has a deep influence on the marketing policy and success of a product (Albaum, Strandskov & Duerr, 2002).

Foreign made goods are considered as high quality products in many countries of the world (Jain, 1989). In Turkey, for example, imported cars are higher quality products than domestic ones. Consumers in Turkey like to buy international automobiles despite the fact that imported cars are much more expensive due to custom duties than local cars. Foreign automakers present the exact same cars to the Turkish market as those in their domestic market. As a result, where international products are considered of higher quality, a standardized marketing strategy is a preferable option (Aydin & Terpstra, 1981). Likewise, the same case applies in Malaysia where foreign made cars are perceived by Malaysians to be better than local made ones.

Marketers can also omit the negative views associated with a country through advertising campaigns (Young, Sauer & Unnara, 1994). For example, Chinese firms presented advertisements in the US channels already being used daily by American consumers to neutralize any biases related to Chinese products.

To summarize, exporting country image has an influential effect on consumer's perception of a product and ultimately companies' marketing strategy. Marketers can overcome the negative image related to the exporting country by adapting their product, price, promotion, and distribution policy in each local market. Thus, it can be assumed that host countries' consumers have a negative view of the country of the manufacturer; hence, it is important for companies and Malaysian exporters to adapt their marketing program policy in international markets.

Depending upon the previous argument, the following research hypotheses are made:

> *Hypothesis 7:* The greater the negative image of the exporting country (Malaysia), the greater the likelihood that Malaysian exporters will adapt their marketing mix strategy.
>
> *H7a:* The greater the negative image of the exporting country (Malaysia), the greater the likelihood that Malaysian exporters will adapt their product strategy to foreign markets.
>
> *H7b:* The greater the negative image of the exporting country (Malaysia), the greater the likelihood that Malaysian exporters will adapt their promotion strategy to foreign markets.
>
> *H7c:* The greater the negative image of the exporting country (Malaysia), the greater the likelihood that Malaysian exporters will adapt their distribution strategy to foreign markets.
>
> *H7d:* The greater the negative image of the exporting country (Malaysia), the greater the likelihood that Malaysian exporters will adapt their pricing strategy to foreign markets.

Physical Conditions

The weather, geography, resources, and size of residential and office buildings are said to be physical conditions of a country (Jain, 1989; Shoham, 1999). Differences in physical conditions between the national and international market affect the feasibility of a standardized marketing policy (Jain, 1989).

Climate conditions also influence the promotion policy of companies (Jeannet & Hennessey, 2001). For example, in the Northern Hemisphere, the winter season is summer season in Southern Hemisphere countries such as Australia, New Zealand, and Argentina. Since sales seasons are performed during the summer vacation of these countries, promotion policy such as TV media and media budget may have to be adapted to cater to the high demand.

In summary, physical conditions such as climate, topography, resources, and size of homes and office buildings affect the extent of adaptation of the marketing policy in foreign markets. It can be assumed that greater differences in physical conditions between local and foreign market will result in a higher degree of marketing program adaptation of companies and Malaysian exporters.

Depending upon the previous assessment, the following research hypotheses are made:

> *Hypothesis 8:* The greater the difference in physical conditions between the local and foreign market, the greater the likelihood that Malaysian exporters will adapt their marketing mix strategy.
> *H8a:* The greater the difference in physical conditions between the local and foreign market, the greater the likelihood that Malaysian exporters will adapt their product strategy in foreign markets.
> *H8b:* The greater the difference in physical conditions between the local and foreign market, the greater the likelihood that Malaysian exporters will adapt their promotion strategy in foreign markets.
> *H8c:* The greater the difference in physical conditions between the local and foreign market, the greater the likelihood that Malaysian exporters will adapt their distribution strategy in foreign markets.
> *H8d:* The greater the difference in physical conditions between the local and foreign market, the greater the likelihood that Malaysian exporters will adapt their pricing strategy in foreign markets.

Marketing Infrastructure

Marketing infrastructure is defined as the "institutions and functions necessary to create, develop, and service demand, including retailers, wholesalers, sales agents, warehousing, transportation, credit, media, and more" (Jain,

1989, p. 75). The extent of standardization of the marketing program is influenced by the accessibility, performance, and cost of the marketing infrastructure in each local market (Jain, 1989).

Absence of marketing infrastructure suppliance in the host market can also forbid companies from using a standardized product policy (Baalbaki & Malhotra, 1993). Unilever, for example, was not capable of presenting frozen vegetables in India, Pakistan, Thailand, and the Philippines since refrigeration facilities were not obtainable at homes and retail stores. Consequently, the company had to roll out dehydrated peas, carrots, and beans (Jain, 1989).

Forbidding the use of a standardized pricing policy is affected by the nature, complexity, and efficiency of the distribution system in a foreign country (Baalbaki & Malhotra, 1993). In countries where the channel structure is ineffective, a uniform pricing strategy cannot be taken since extra distribution costs will be added to the price of the product (Jain, 1989). In countries where discount stores are not common, companies may not be capable of using a price penetration policy, thus forbidding the use of a standardized pricing policy (Douglas & Craig, 1986). For instance, prepared foods were respectively most expensive in Italy, followed by Germany and the Netherlands. The price difference across the three above mentioned countries was because of the different retail structure (Jain, 1989).

Chung (2003) conducted a study that attempted to examine the international standardization strategies in which the experiences of Australian and New Zealand firms operating in the greater China markets were investigated. The findings of Chung's (2003) study revealed that Marketing infrastructure in host countries were considered by to be an important determinant of their standardization/adaptation strategies. A number of other researchers used Chung's (2003) findings regarding the relationship between marketing infrastructure and standardization/adaptation strategies to support their hypotheses regarding this relationship. In this context, Hise (2010) conducted a study that attempted to investigate whether US companies employing standardization or adaptation strategies in their international markets. Hise (2010) depended on Chnug's (2003) findings regarding the relationship between marketing infrastructure and standardization/adaptation strategies hypothesizing that Marketing infrastructure in host countries will be considered by the respondent food companies to be an important determinant of their standardization/adaptation strategies.

In short, marketing infrastructure affects all trends of the marketing program and the extent of standardization. Differences between countries in terms of the marketing infrastructure will compel exporting companies to adapt their marketing policy. One can also claim that differences in marketing infrastructure between home and export market will compel Malaysian exporters to alter their marketing strategy.

Depending upon the previous discussion, the following research hypotheses are made:

> *Hypothesis 9:* The greater the difference between the marketing infrastructure of the exporters' local and foreign market, the greater the likelihood that Malaysian exporters will adapt their marketing mix strategy.
> *H9a:* The greater the difference between the marketing infrastructure of the exporters' local and foreign market, the greater the level of adaptation of the product strategy of Malaysian exporters.
> *H9b:* The greater the difference between the marketing infrastructure of the exporters' local and foreign market, the greater the level of adaptation of the promotion strategy of Malaysian exporters.
> *H9c:* The greater the difference between the marketing infrastructure of the exporters' local and foreign market, the greater the level of adaptation of the distribution strategy of Malaysian exporters.
> *H9d:* The greater the difference between the marketing infrastructure of the exporters' local and foreign market, the greater the level of adaptation of the pricing strategy of Malaysian exporters.

In the literature on studying the impact of the antecedent factors on the marketing mix adaptation, a number of research studies should different results raging from low to high impact and some studies even showed negative relationship between the antecedent factors and marketing mix adaptation. The following table (Table 2.1) presents a summary of these findings.

The Mediating Effects of the Marketing Mix

Many research studies examined the direct effects of the antecedent factors on the marketing mix adaptation strategies (Cavusgil *et al.*, 1993; Johnson & Arunthanes, 1995; Park, 200). Other research studies attempted to examine the impact of the marketing mix strategies on the export performance of companies (Kostova, Roth & Dacin, 2008; Nigam & Su, 2010; Alvi, 2012). However, limited research has been conducted on the mediating influence of marketing mix on the relationship between the antecedent factors and export performance. This particular influence is regarded as one of the main contributions the present research hopes to achieve. Thus, one of the main objectives in the present research is to examine the mediating effect of marketing mix on the relationship between the antecedent factors (Independent Variables) and the export performance of Malaysian companies (Dependent Variable).

Table 2.1: Summary of Determinants and Degree of Marketing Strategy Adaptation

Determinants	*Extent*	*Degree of Adaptation of the Marketing Strategy*	*Illustrative Studies*
International Experience	More Experience	High	Aaby & Slater (1989), Cavusgil & Kirpalani (1993), Cavusgil & Zou (1994), Chetty & Hamilton (1993).
Technology Intensity	High	High/Low Adaptation of — Marketing Strategy — Low Product Adaptation — Low Promotion Adaptation — High Price Adaptation High Distribution Adaptation	Cavusgil & Zou (1994), Chetty & Hamilton (1993), Stewart & McAuley (2000), Zou & Stan (1998).
Competition Level	High	High	Aaby & Slater (1989), Cavusgil & Zou (1994), Chetty & Hamilton (1993), De Luz (1993).
Government Regulations	Greater Difference	High	Aaby & Slater (1989), Chetty & Hamilton (1993), De Luz (1993), Stewart & McAuley (2000).
Cultural Differences	Greater Difference	High	Aaby & Slater (1989), Cavusgil & Kirpalani (1993), Cavusgil & Zou (1994).
Economic Differences	Greater Difference	High	Chetty & Hamilton (1993), De Luz (1993), Koh & Robicheaux (1988), Stewart & McAuley (2000).
Exporting Country Image	Negative	High	Koh & Robicheaux (1988), Stewart & McAuley (2000), Zou & Stan (1998).
Physical Conditions	Greater Difference	High	Cavusgil & Kirpalani (1993), Cavusgil & Zou (1994), Chetty & Hamilton (1993).
Marketing Infrastructure’	Greater Difference	High	Cavusgil & Kirpalani (1993), Cavusgil & Zou (1994), Chetty & Hamilton (1993), De Luz (1993), Koh & Robicheaux (1988).

Despite the scarcity of the research conducted on the mediating influence of marketing mix, a number of researchers recommended that this mediating effect should be examined in future work (Lages & Montgomery, 2001; Park, 2006). Based on this discussion, the following hypotheses are generated:

> *Hypothesis 10:* The firm marketing mix mediates the relationship between the firm antecedents and the performance of Malaysian export companies
>
> *H10.1:* The marketing mix adaptation mediates the effect of international experience on the performance of Malaysian export companies
>
> *H10.2:* The marketing mix adaptation mediates the effect of technology intensity on the performance of Malaysian export companies.
>
> *H10.3:* The marketing mix adaptation mediates the effect of competition level of the industry on performance of Malaysian export companies.
>
> *Hy10.4:* The marketing mix adaptation mediates the effect of differences of government regulations between home and export market on performance of Malaysian export companies.
>
> *H10.5:* The marketing mix adaptation mediates the effect of cultural differences between home and export market on performance of Malaysian export companies
>
> *H10.6:* The marketing mix adaptation mediates the effect of economic differences between the home market and foreign market on performance of Malaysian export companies.
>
> *H10.7:* The marketing mix adaptation mediates the effect of the country image of the exporting country on performance of Malaysian export companies.
>
> *H10.8:* The marketing mix adaptation mediates the effect of differences in physical conditions between the exporters' home market and foreign market on performance of Malaysian export companies.
>
> *H10.9:* The marketing mix adaptation mediates the effect of differences in marketing infrastructure between the exporters' home market and foreign market on performance of Malaysian export companies

Marketing Mix (Adaptation) and Organizational Performance

Alvi (2012) asserts that contemporary literature advocates for broader analyses of firms' institutional frameworks, and contexts for purposes of bettering the way they adapt strategies in economies that are emerging. In his study, he investigates the cognitive difficulties that may hinder the appreciation of the contexts. He reveals that unwittingly, businesspeople, in thinking through adaptation issues, are inclined towards crafting the related strategies on the basis of their preferred emerging markets' configurations as opposed to what the configurations really are. Wang, Jaw and Huang (2008) indicate that investigations of the performance of any firm that has operations in both the emerging as well as the advanced markets should look at control theory, institutionalism, perspectives of resource reliance, and institutionalism aspects. The aspects should especially be considered in investigating the determinants, cross-culture and strategic control of global human resources in the firms' subsidiaries (Wang, Jaw & Huang, 2008).

In their findings, Wang, Jaw and Huang (2008) demonstrate that firms that employ adaptation strategies experience growth in their profitability if the design of their input control allows for ample response to both high adaptations along with high integration. On the other hand, their behavioral control ought to be responsive to low levels of adaptation and high levels of integration. These responses should run concurrently where the activities of the subsidiaries are of low value (Wang, Jaw & Huang, 2008). According to Kostova Roth and Dacin (2008), much of the extant literature on how firms can better adjust to the local emerging market condition point out what specifically the firms should adapt to: tastes and climatic differences, nature of the available infrastructure, and spending capacity, among others. Firms see an increase in their profitability if they adapt well to them, in ways that are responsive. Adaptation, as a strategy, is seen as being responsive if it keen on the extant deep context, its design is particular to the realities at hand, and affords the firms the advantages of exceptional approaches, which are adequately idiosyncratic (Kostova, Roth & Dacin, 2008).

A meta-analytical approach in reviewing literature adds to the literature's growth on a given subject, and promotes its capacity for being generalized inapplicability. In their study, Brei, D'Avila, Camargo and Engels (2011) employ this approach. They note that the extant literature on adaptation, as it relates to firms' performance and related concerns, is limited. In reviewing literature, five of the articles that they analyzed showed that adaptation occasions a high level of performance in the firms that employ it. Six articles showed that the adaption had no significant impact or adversely impacted on the performance. The correlation of the hypothesis that the firms' product adaptation in the emerging markets or other external environs improves performance is 0.154 and is thus accepted. The correlation related to the comparable hypotheses on promotion adaptation is 0.155, distribution is 0.141, and price is 0.209. The correlations thus confirm all the hypotheses. The various forms of adaptations affect firms' performances positively (Brei, D'Avila, Camargo & Engels, 2011).

Enderwick (2009) concludes that firms that are underperforming or experiencing problematic commercial environs should adapt. Their adaptation should be in ways that are non-incremental, so as to boost their performances and ensure their survival. The adaptation approaches should take into consideration any anticipated essential changes. Enderwick (2009) notes that the exposure of firms to emerging market's dynamics can persuade them to adapt. By adapting, the firms become highly competitive in the face of the dynamics. In conducting a literature review, Nigam and Su (2010) identify various gaps in how a centralized management of a firm carries out its mandate and how subsidiary managements carry out theirs. Firms ought to adapt to the existing gaps and related differences so as to enhance their performance according to Nigam and Su (2010).

Nigam and Su (2010) put forth the proposition that the more the firms in emerging economies appreciate and, accordingly, adapt to the institutional frameworks of their host economies, the higher their organizational performance especially in relation to their human resource-related policies. A need for adaption by firms within emerging countries has been established by Yeung (2008). He notes that by adapting, the firms heighten their performance as they become more focused on their core capacities and competencies, rationalizing their commercial units so as to leverage their primary strengths for building market headship. Stefan & Thomas (2011) present a theoretical construct coalesced with the situation-strategy fit concept regarding adaptation as well as standardization, and contends that standardization more strongly enhances the performance of firms that have operations in emerging economies compared to other strategies, including adaptation.

Powers and Loyka (2010), through a survey, make out the degree to which individual elements of marketing mix are or become adapted. The data that they collected shows that the adaptation of products, prices, promotion, as well as distribution is essential in increasing firms' performance (Powers & Loyka, 2010). Hieu and Truong (2010), using an comparative analysis of case studies, show that two firms, registered in Italy, but having their manufacturing operations domiciled in Vietnam, use both standardization along with adaptation in ensuring that their performance remains favorable. Though the two firms benefit from both strategies in terms of their performances, the extents to which they do that vary significantly. In the study by Hieu and Truong (2010), the level of contribution of adaptation to the performances of the firms is not explicitly stated.

Stefan & Thomas (2011) demonstrate that global product standardization universally improves the profitability of the product in foreign markets, including emerging markets. To ensure high performance of products as well as firms, the standardization should allow for the emergence of high international demand homogeneity, and elasticity in respect of the products, small managers' perceptual fault, and a polished execution plan for the strategy (Stefan & Thomas, 2011). Aviv, Makovec, Vesna and Ayalla (2008) contend that majority of the extant research on the subject of standardization explores marketing mix contexts. There is minimal research on standardization in the context of management characteristics and processes. The data that they gathered via a Slovenia-based survey shows that the characteristics and processes within the global control of distribution channels heighten firms' performances. Standardization also positively impacts on the firm's behavioral outcomes (Aviv, Makovec, Vesna & Ayalla, 2008).

Brei, D'Avila, Camargo and Engels (2011) present hypotheses linking firms' performances and marketing mix. The linkage is partly moderated by variables of standardization. The statistical correlation of the hypothesis that product standardization in markets, including emerging ones, positively affects firms' performance is 0.134 and thus is accepted. The correlations with respect to promotion is 0.134, distribution is 0.133, and price is also 0.133. These correlations confirm that standardization, with respect to product, distribution, price, and promotion, improves the performance of the firms that apply it. The correlations are quite comparable to one another as the hypotheses are similar (Brei, D'Avila, Camargo & Engels, 2011).

Pudelko and Harzing (2008) assert that among the most intricate difficulties that multinational firms have to contend with, relate to the harmonization of the contrasting forces of localization, on the one hand, and standardization on the other. They demonstrate that firms' performances are high if they adopt standardization, especially standardization that leans towards international best practices, as opposed to leaning toward headquarters' localization practices. The firms' subsidiaries benefit from global knowledge and learning, which are essential in ensuring high performance, regardless of where the knowledge and learning are domiciled (Pudelko & Harzing, 2008). Aybar (2012) sampled 54 firms, which have ADR concerns within the US, from nine emerging countries in a study on the effects of standardization of their corporate governance practices and mechanisms on performance. Aybar (2012) obtained accounting-related data from DataStream International, and used it to determine their performances. Governance-related data was obtained from Standard and Poor's. He concludes that firms that adopt the global standards of corporate governance are appreciably profitable and valuable (Aybar, 2012).

Rocha and Silva (2011) demonstrate that firms that employ standardization as a strategy perform highly. This is especially so for companies that face competition in international scopes, in market segments like those for perfumes and fashion whose market reaches are global. They present the proposition that the standardization or centralization of decisions relate to product variables and decisions that are not related to products increase performance.

Standardization of actions and policies significantly lessens the risks associated with subsidiary staff errors. Such staff may be deficient in specialized skills and information. Standardization allows managements to have a close control of all firms' decisions and operations, including in the subsidiaries. Rocha and Silva (2011) affirm that standardization is closely related to centralization.

Standardization ensures strong coordination and control between subsidiaries and headquarters, thus firming the firms' performances (Rocha & Silva, 2011). Kustin (2010) explores the question of whether there are benefits to the strategies, and thus profitability, of firms' standardization of marketing. Kustin (2010) establishes that there is mounting support for strategies for ensuring the standardization of components of marketing mix and adding to their profit-linked performance of the firms. Sheth (2011) asserts that for firms to accommodate the contemporary characteristics of emerging markets and perform highly, they ought to rethink the classical perspectives on marketing to market standardization and aggregation, from differential advantages.

According to Schilke and Thomas (2009), standardization of programs of marketing attracts appreciable attention from researchers. They agree with the shared finding in previous research that standardization improves a firm's performance and performance-related outcomes. Upon surveying 489 companies, they establish that the linkage between performance and standardization is more pronounced in firms that are large and with offerings of products that are homogeneous, whose international market penetration is high, and that employ a strategy of cost-leadership. To realize high performance, the firms ought to also have strong capabilities for coordination. Vrontis, Thrassou and Lamprianou (2009) and Ryans, Griffith and Jain (2008) concur that to perform highly, firms in emerging economies should adopt a favorable mix of standardization and adaptation, without excluding either of them. The two studies indicate that both improve performance in the firms that adopt and actualize them.

A number of researchers attempted to study the relationships between market mix and export performance and these researchers reported different findings regarding these relationships. Some researchers reported a positive relationship between market mix and export performance (Lages & Lages, 2004; Eusebio, Andreu & Bleze, 2007; Mavrogiannis *et al.*, 2008; Lages, Silva & Styles, 2009; Tantong, Krande, Nair & Singhapakdi, 2010; Morgan, Kaleka & Katsikeas, 2004). Other studies, however, reported a negative relationship between elements of market mix and export performance (Lages, Jose & Cristiana, 2008). Furthermore, it has been reported by some research studies that no relationship was found between elements of marketing mix and export performance (Leonidou, Katsikeas & Samiee, 2002; Abdul-Adis & Md. Sidin, 2010; Eusebio *et al.*, 2007).

Based on the discussions above, the following four hypotheses are generated. These hypotheses address the influence of marketing mix (adaptation) on the performance of Malaysian export companies:

> *Hypothesis 11:* The greater the firm's level of marketing mix strategy adaptation, the better the Malaysian exporters' performance.
> *Hypothesis 11a:* The greater the level of product strategy adaptation, the better the Malaysian exporters' performance.
> *Hypothesis 11b:* The greater the level of promotion strategy adaptation, the better the Malaysian exporters' performance.
> *Hypothesis 11c:* The greater the level of distribution strategy adaptation, the better the Malaysian exporters' performance.
> *Hypothesis 11d:* The greater the level of pricing strategy adaptation, the better the Malaysian exporters' performance.

EMPIRICAL RESULTS

An overview of the Table 2.5 suggests that empirical results of the antecedent factors of the degree of adaptation of the marketing mix are inconclusive. Such result can be interpreted in terms of the use of different indicators or single item measures to determine the same construct across various studies. The operationalization of the same construct varies from one single measure item to another.

Many studies utilize perceived extent of management's international experience, the number of years the company possess in international business, and also the number of foreign companies where the company has ongoing operations as proxies of the level of international experience. Among these studies, three found that the degree of marketing mix adaptation is associated with the amount of international experience (Cavusgil & Zou, 1994; Cavusgil, Zou & Naidu, 1993; Chung, 2003), while one found no significant affect between the two (Chung, 2002).

Many studies employ cultural likelihood of export market to local market, understanding and interpretation of advertisement, consumer literacy and education level, linguistic and connotative implications, and socio-cultural customs and taboos. One study claims that similarity of culture between the home and export market was essentially related to the degree of marketing mix adaptation (Chung, 2003) whereas another one finds no important relationship between the two variables (Johnson & Arunthanes, 1995).

Several studies employ difference between export and local market on distribution institutions, warehousing, transport service capabilities, distribution infrastructure, and media availability as proxies of marketing infrastructure. One study claims that there is an essential influence of difference

Table 2.2: Empirical Results

Author(s)	*Sample*	*Dependent Variable(s)*	*Independent Variable(s)*	*Findings*
Akaah (1991)	US firms	Product, pricing, distribution, promotion, and marketing management process standardization	Consumer characteristics and behaviour, environmental characteristics, competitive environment, nature of ownership and corporate orientation	— Firms tend to standardize their marketing strategy if customers in the US and host country are similar in terms of characteristics and behaviour. — Firms tend to standardize their marketing process adaptation if they possess ownership interest in the host country operations. — Geocentric/regiocentric firms standardize their marketing strategy more than ethnocentric/ polycentric firms.
Cavusgil & Zou (1994)	US exporters	Product and promotion adaptation, support to foreign distributor/ subsidiary and price competitiveness and performance	International experience, commitment to venture, cultural specificity of product, product uniqueness, firm's experience with product, technology intensity, export market competitiveness and brand familiarity of export customers	— International experience, commitment to venture, cultural specificity, product uniqueness, firm's experience with product, technology intensity, export market competitiveness and brand familiarity of export customers have a significant effect on product and promotion adaptation, support to foreign distributor/subsidiary and price competitiveness. — Product and promotion adaptation support to foreign distributor/subsidiary and price competitiveness, international experience, and commitment to venture have a significant effect on export marketing performance.
Cavusgil *et al.* (1993)	US exporters	Product and promotion adaptation	Technology intensiveness, product uniqueness, cultural specificity of product, type of product, international experience, export sales goal, entry scope, similarity of legal regulations, competitiveness of export market and product familiarity of export customers.	— International experience, sales goal, entry scope, product type, cultural specificity of product, product uniqueness, technology intensity, similarity of regulations, export market competitiveness, and product familiarity have a significant effect on product and/or promotion adaptation.

Table 2.2 *(Contd.)*

Author(s)	*Sample*	*Dependent Variable(s)*	*Independent Variable(s)*	*Findings*
Chung (2002)	Australia & New Zealand Exporters	Extent of adaptation of product, price, promotion, place and performance	International business experience, market entry mode, immigrant effect, government regulations, economic development, marketing environment, product type and product life cycle	— Economic development had significant effect on distribution adaptation. — Competitive environment had a significant effect on distribution, promotion and price adaptation. — Government regulations had a significant effect on distribution and product adaptation. — Immigration effect had a significant effect on promotion, product and price adaptation.
Chung (2003)	Australian & New Zealand Exporters	Extent of product, price, place, promotion, and marketing process standardization and performance	Firm size, marketing infrastructure, entry mode effect, economic environment, political/legal environment, cultural environment, international business experience, competitive environment and product type	— Firm size, political/legal environment, cultural environment, international business experience, competitive environment, and product type had a significant effect on the marketing mix standardization. — Product and place standardization have a significant effect on export performance.
Johnson & Arunthanes (1995)	US exporters	Product adaptation and performance	Government regulation, infrastructure differences, market lag, competitive intensity, type of product, cultural differences and end-user differences in preferences and tastes	— Product adaptation is significantly greater for consumer products than that of industrial products. — Government regulations significantly affect product adaptation. — Infrastructure differences lead to higher adaptation of consumer products than industrial products. — Product adaptation has no effect on profits.
Lages & Montgomery (2001)	Portuguese exporters	Firm's current year	Competition in the industry and commerce.	— Export performance has a significant effect on product adaptation.

of marketing infrastructure on marketing mix policy adaptation (Chung, 2003). However, three of these studies find that there is no important relationship between the two variables (Akaah, 1991; Cavusgil & Zou; 1994; Johnson & Arunthanes, 1995; Shoham, 1999). The following table (Table 2.6) represents some empirical results from the literature.

EXPORT PERFORMANCE

In the assessment of the suitability of a specific strategy, performance is generally the top most important consideration. However, despite its importance in international marketing strategy, performance has only been given limited empirical attention (Jain, 1989), especially in an MNC context where the results are contradictory and inconclusive. A suitable strategy for a specific firm hinges on the context in which the plan has been implemented (Dess, Lumpkin, and Covin, 1997; Miller, 1986; Naman and Slevin, 1993). This is timely evidence for those MNCs located in emerging countries and are struggling for growth, development and success in an age where there is rampant globalization of markets and intense competition worldwide.

According to Katsikeas *et al.* (2000) & Shoham (1999, 1996), export performance is considered to be the outcome of a firm's export activities. Present findings confirm that firm and marketing environmentally linked factors can have a critical effect on the firm's performance (Cavusgil *et al.*, 1993; Zou & Cavusgil, 2002; O'Cass & Julian, 2003, Chung, 2007). Nevertheless, there is still some variation in the literature regarding conceptual and operational definitions (Aaby & Slater, 1989; Madsen, 1987; Shoham, 1999). According to literature, a marketing strategy will only be able to produce excellent performance when implemented properly and effectively (Vorhies and Morgan, 2003). Another evidence points to the fact that it is imperative to keep in mind that the challenges that exporters face are generally linked to the controllable issues stemming from the internal environment (Stefan & Thomas, 2011).

In addressing how marketing strategies influence performance, Ang and Massingham (2007) argue that the company's decision as whether to standardize or adapt its strategies (product, promotion, distribution, or pricing) is fundamental. This is because such decisions influence the organization's fundamental approach to business and how it will compete in a highly competitive environment. For example, those who support the standardization strategy believe that the world is becoming more and more globalised and homogeneous, taking into account the outcome of the advancements in communication and technology (Jain, 1989). Consequently, tastes and cultures of consumers around the globe are becoming homogeneous and these consumers now share preferences, needs, desires and demands (Vrontis &

Papasolomou, 2005; Jain, 1989, 2007). Such similarity of preferences, demands, and needs between consumers from different part of the world now make it possible for organisations to produce more standardized products using standardized marketing strategy (Zou & Cavusgil, 2002).

Evidence from the literature review also reveals that export performance is related to both internal and external factors of firms. The internal factors that influence firm's export performance include marketing strategy, product and firm characteristics organizational structure, managerial experience, and resource availability (Barney, 1991; Christensen, Darocha & Gertner, 1987; Culpan, 1989; Da Rocha & Christensen, 1994; Da Rocha, Cristensen & Da Cunha, 1990; Dichtl, Koglmayr & Muller, 1990; Katsikeas et al, 2000; Cavusgil & Zou, 1994; Cavusgil *et al.*, 1993; Cooper & Kleinschmidt, 1985; Leonidou *et al.*, 2002). External factors for firm's export performance include industry competitiveness, industry and market characteristics business environment, or product characteristics (Bain, 1968; Cavusgil & Zou, 1994, Cavusgil *et al.*, 1993; Leonidou *et al.*, 2002; Cooper & Kleinschmidt, 1985; Leonidou *et al.*, 2002). Calantone, Kim, Schmidt & Cavusgil (2006) state the lack of literature pertaining to cross-cultural differences in a firm's export performance

Based on the theoretical developments in the light of multidimensional assessment of business performance (e.g., Morgan, Kaleka and Katsikeas, 2004), performance of the company consists of market performance, revealing economic marketing indicators on sales and market share; financial performance, encapsulating the venture's profitability and return on investment; and customer performance, which is linked to the venture's response to customer needs and pressures in the market.

MALAYSIA AND EXPORTING ACTIVITIES

Malaysia, ranks among the nations in the Pacific Rim, that has gone through rapid development and economic growth; the country is considered as a role model for successful economic development by world bodies such as World Bank and the International Monetary Fund. The growth in Malaysia can be attributed to the state-oriented market economy, whereby the government has a significant role in guiding economic activity plans. The Malaysian economy ranked 3rd in 2007 in Southeast Asia and 29th in the world, measured by purchasing power parity (CIA, 2008). International trade has a significant role in Malaysian economy and over three decades, Malaysia has undergone a major economic development owing to its outward looking strategies. Similar to first-generation tigers comprising Korea, Taiwan, Singapore and Hong Kong, Malaysia has used the exports propeller of growth and development since the 1970. It is interesting to note that Malaysia's economy even continued to grow after the 1997 economic crisis in an environment of low inflation and rampant unemployment.

Malaysia's development is guided by a series of five-year development plans; the country's economy transformed from being a commodity exporter to manufacturing exporter. Back in the 1970s, Malaysia was well-known as the largest producer of tin, rubber and palm oil at the global level. Recently, manufacturing has largely come into play in the country's economic development and Malaysia has transformed from import substitution to a liberal outward-oriented trade regime (Shazali Abu Mansor *et al.*, 2000). Manufacturing accounts for 79 per cent of the total export earnings and nearly 29 per cent of Malaysia's Gross Domestic Product (GDP) (Chandran V.G.R. *et al.*, 2003). Additionally, this particular sector replaced agriculture as the top sector contributing to the economy, playing a decisive role in Malaysia's development and success. It has contributed to the output, employment and exports. The export sector has been recently in the forefront in the transformation of the Malaysian economy and has made the country a significant world exporter of semi-conductors, air-conditioners and latex-dipped goods. Owing to the positive signs of solid economic revival stemming from the major economies of the world, Malaysia's imports-exports is expected to grow even further. Other elements that contribute to the growing economy are: the improvement in business, the sentiments of the residents, domestic demand particularly in private consumption and the increase in investments led by the private sector.

Not surprisingly, Malaysia now holds a major position in ASEAN markets as in the year 2008, the total amount of its exports to ASEAN countries increased to RM171.19 billion which accounted for a 10 per cent increase. About 25.8 per cent of Malaysia's total exports in 2008 were to ASEAN. Malaysia reported a trade surplus of RM 12.5 billion in March 2009, making it the 137th consecutive month that recorded the trade surplus since November 1997. Malaysia's major exports include electrical and electronic goods, liquefied natural gas (LNG), palm oil and related products, petroleum and related products, timber and timber based products, chemicals and metals while major export destinations for Malaysian goods include Japan, China, USA, Singapore, South Korea, Thailand, India, Australia, Hong Kong and England which account for 71.8 per cent of Malaysia's exports (2009).

MALAYSIAN EXPORTS

Several government agencies in several ministries facilitate Malaysia's exporting activities. These government agencies are MATRADE—Malaysia Trade Development Corporation, MITI—Ministry of International Trade and Industry, SIRIM—Standards and Industrial Research Institute of Malaysia,

FMM—Federation of Malaysian Manufacturers, CCI—Chamber of Commerce and Industry, SMI—Small and Medium Industries, SMIDEC—Small and Medium Industries Development Corporation. The total number of Malaysian exporting companies that appeared in these agencies is nearly 3000 exporting firms. These firms have various experience levels ranging from one year to over twenty years of exporting experience.

1. *Malaysia External Trade Development Corporation (MATRADE):* MATRADE is a government agency established on March 1, 1993 to act as the external trade promotion branch of Malaysia's MITI. MATRADE aims to help Malaysia take its place as one of the global competitive trading nations, while facilitating the country's enterprises' promotion globally (Matrade, 2009). MATRADE has the following functions:

- To advertise, facilitate and improve Malaysia's external trade with a concentration on the export of manufactured and semi-manufactured products as well as services.
- To develop and set up export marketing strategies and trade promotion activities in order to promote Malaysia's exports.
- To carry out commercial intelligence and market research in order to create a comprehensive database of information to improve and develop Malaysia's trade.
- To set up training programs in order to improve international marketing skills of Malaysian exporters.
- To achieve an improvement and also to protect Malaysia's international trade investment overseas.
- To advertise, assist and also set up service areas that are related to trade.

MATRADE works as a main organization for Malaysian exporters and foreign importers for the purpose of collecting trade-related information. MATRADE provides market intelligence and relevant advice to assist Malaysian exporters to improve their products and services in the highly competitive global markets. This results in smooth and efficient processes of international trade. Also, MATRADE facilitates the search for possibilities of overseas markets for Malaysian products and services with the help of its international network consisting of 38 overseas offices in important commercial cities all over the globe. MATRADE's activities include the following.

(a) Matching foreign buyers with value added products and services of Malaysian exporters;
(b) Setting up trade missions and participation of Malaysian exporters in international trade exhibitions;

(c) Conducting seminars as well as workshops regarding trade opportunities and processes, regulations and procedures, as well as international marketing issues;
(d) Supplying and distributing up-to-date trade information and market intelligence;
(e) Overseeing exhibitions on Made in Malaysia products.

2. *Ministry of International Trade and Industry (MITI):* MITI has been established for the following purposes:

(a) Advertise and strategize Malaysia's global competitiveness in the international arena through the production of high value added goods and services;
(b) Enforce the development of industrial activities towards the enhancement of Malaysia's economic growth to achieve a developed nation status by 2020;
(c) Draw up, legislate and enforce international trade and industrial policies that will guarantee Malaysia's quick development towards the achievement of the National Economic Policy and Vision 2020.

Moreover, MITI also acts as an agency that:

- Plans, formulates and implements policies on industrial development, international trade and investment.
- Encourages foreign and domestic investment.
- Promotes Malaysia's exports of manufacturing products and services by strengthening bilateral, multilateral and regional trade relations and cooperation
- Enhances national productivity and competitiveness in the manufacturing sector.

3. *Standard and Industrial Research Institute of Malaysia (SIRIM):* SIRIM is a government-owned company under the umbrella of the Ministry of Finance which acts as the national organization of standardization and quality. Additionally, it is the prime mover in industrial research and development, which assist in manifesting national dynamism through technological expertise and global acceptance of Malaysian products and service. SIRIM's mission is to improve customer's competitiveness with the help of technology quality and satisfy the needs of its shareholders.

In sum, SIRIM's role is to act as:

- A champion of quality;
- The national technology development corporation;
- Vehicle for technology transfer;

- A provider of institutional and technical infrastructure for the Government.

Some of the functions of SIRIM include:

- promoting and undertaking scientific industrial research;
- boosting industrial efficiency and development;
- providing technology transfer and consultancy services;
- developing Malaysian standards and promoting standardization and quality assurance for greater competitiveness;
- enhancing public and industrial welfare, health and safety.

4. *Federation of Malaysian Manufacturers (FMM)*: The Federation of Malaysian Manufacturers (FMM) is considered as Malaysia's premier organization. The federation was established in 1968 and has been consistently leading Malaysian Manufacturers in the development of the nation.

Currently, it is regarded as the largest private sector economic organization in Malaysia. Included in its list are more than 3,000 manufacturing and industrial service companies of different sizes. In addition, FMM is now being recognized as the voice of the industry; since its inception, it has been constantly working with the Malaysian manufacturing sector as its representative body for over 36 years. Moreover, FMM is an ISO9001: 2000 certified company limited by guarantee. Leading FMM are the captains of industry, Council and State Branches, issues-oriented Working Committees and Industry Groups, etc. FMM represents the manufacturing sector at international, regional, national, state, local authorities and industry sub-sector levels. Furthermore, FMM provides a variety of services and activities in order to assist in business operations.

Conveniently published in Malaysia, the FMM directory is the most established and authoritative directory, providing a comprehensive profile of Malaysian industries, and a wide range of information necessary for business dealings. It also facilitates widespread advertisements locally and abroad.

In sum, Malaysian firms depend on different resources for their export products' successful promotion. These sources comprise informal business contacts, MATRADE, business publications, foreign embassies, export seminars–sources that are crucial in guaranteeing the success of their exporting promotional activities. The above sources provide much-needed and invaluable information that is useful and effective in helping to facilitate the firm's competency in export promotion and in providing firms with competitive advantage. Along the same lines, firms desiring to succeed in product promotion abroad, particularly in emerging markets, are normally advised to utilize a combination of the above sources for information collection (Yip, 2003).

RESEARCH FRAMEWORK

Based on the previous section on research hypotheses and the antecedent factors influencing the degree of adaptation of firms, the following figure (Figure 2.1) shows the framework upon which the study is grounded. This framework is grounded on previous research studies that have been conducted in the field of marketing mix (Jain, 1989; Cavusgil & Zou, 1994; Cavusgil, Zou & Naidu, 1993; Chung, 2002; Shoham, 1999; Park, 2006). Park (2006) argues that the degree of marketing adaptation is a function of a group of firm factors (e.g., international experience), industry factors (e.g., technology intensity, level of competition), and export market factors (e.g., government regulation, cultural differences, economic differences, physical conditions, and marketing infrastructure). It also suggests that the degree of overall marketing strategy adaptation is influenced by the many internal (firm and product factors) and external (industry and export market factors) factors.

The unique characteristics of the suggested framework is that it includes not only the most important factors that decide the degree of adaptation/ standardization of marketing mix but also deletes the findings of the extant literature in a non-Western context (i.e., Malaysia). The present research is similar to one conducted by Park (2006) in the sense that most of the factors that were used on Park's study were adopted for the current research. Specifically, the factors that have been adopted to influence the marketing mix in the present research include international experience, technology intensity, competition level, government regulation, cultural differences, economic differences, country image, physical condition, and marketing infrastructure.

Before introducing the framework upon which this study is grounded, it was thought it would be good to highlight the antecedent factors that have been hypothesized to influence the overall marketing mix in the export field. To make it easier to comprehend, the previous researchers together with the factors that have been suggested and used in their studies are presented in the following Table 2.3.

Thus, based on these previous studies and Park's (2006) study in particular, the framework designed for this study is grounded. The following Figure 2.1 represents the framework of the current research.

It can be seen from the framework figure above (Figure 2.1) that it consists of three main variables, namely independent variables, mediating variable and finally the dependent variable. Here, the antecedent factors of international experience, technology intensity, competition level, government regulation, cultural differences, economic differences, country image, physical condition, and marketing infrastructure make up the independent variables. On the other hand, the four adaptation strategies of promotion adaptation, product

Table 2.3: Previous Studies on the Antecedents Factors

Dimensions	*Cavusgil & Zou (1994)*	*Chung (2002)*	*Jain (1989)*	*Shoam (1999)*	*Park (2006)*
Firm Factors	— International Experience — Commitment to the venture — International Business Intensity	— International Experience — Market entry mode — Immigrant effect	— Corporate orientation — Delegation of authority		— International Experience
Product Factors	— Cultural Specificity of the product. — Product Uniqueness — Firms' experience with the product — Product's technical complexity	— Nature of product — Product life cycle	— Type of product — Product positioning		— Type of product
Industry Factors	— Technology Intensiveness — Intensity of price competition	— Competitive environment	— Competition	— Competitive position — Competition Structure	— Technology Intensity — Competition Level
Export Market Factors	— Export market attractiveness — Cultural/legal similarity of the product — Export market competitive intensity — Brand familiarity of export customers.	— Government regulation — Economic development	— Market development — Market condition — Physical environment — Legal environment — Market infrastructure — Geographic area	— Country image — Law differences — Government Influence — Physical Climate — Market infrastructure	— Government regulation — Cultural Differences — Economic development — Export country image — Physical condition — Market infrastructure
Sample	US Exporters	New Zealand	US Exporters	Israeli Exporters	Korean Exporters

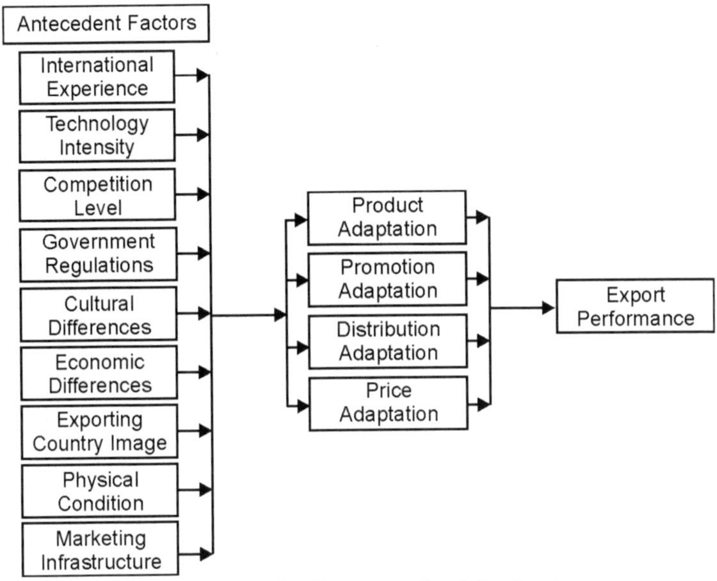

Figure 2.1: The Framework of the Study

adaptation, distribution adaptation and price adaptation (Marketing Mix) make up the mediating variables. Finally export performance makes up the dependent variable. In this study, an attempt is first made to examine the relationship between the antecedent factors (independent variables) and marketing mix (mediating variable). After that, the relationship between the marketing mix (mediating variable) and export performance (dependent variable) will be investigated. These two links have been explored in the literature by a number of researchers (Shoham, 1999; Leonidou, *et al.*, 2002; Park, 2006; Mavrogiannis, Bourlakis, Dawson & Mitchell, 2008; Tantong, *et al.*, 2010). The present research takes a step further by examining a third link, namely the link between the antecedent factors (independent variables) and export performance (dependent variable) through the mediating influence of marketing mix (mediating variable). This link has not been explored in the literature particularly in an emerging country context, and the link has been investigated once in the literature by Park (2006) but in Park's study, the impact on the antecedent factors on export performance has been examined through the mediating influence of marketing mix individually where the mediating impact of each of the four adaptation strategies has been examined separately. In this study, however, the mediating impact of the adaptation mix as a whole will be examined.

Three
Research Methodology

The main aim of this study is to examine the degree of adaptation of Malaysian firms in their marketing strategies and export performance. For the purpose of achieving such an objective, a number of methodical issues have to be clarified so that the findings can be conclusively determined. Hence, this study clarifies issues regarding the research methodology, the research design, instrument, construct, population, sampling and finally data analysis.

RESEARCH DESIGN

This research attempts to present the adaptation degrees of Malaysian firms in their marketing strategies and export performance. Therefore, the research design adopted to help achieve this goal is the quantitative research design. In this way, Malaysian firms are investigated particularly regarding their marketing strategies and export performance, and constructs for the measurement of these variables are created. A quantitative research design is generally utilized in order to investigate research questions. Quantitative experiments normally use a standard format with only a few exceptional cases, particularly minor inter-disciplinary differences of generating a hypothesis to be proved or disproved. The main goal is to classify features, count them, and construct statistical models for the purpose of explaining what has been observed. The hypothesis is relevant only when it can be proven through mathematical and statistical means and will become the basis through which the whole research is designed.

A quantitative research design is an effective way of finalizing the results and proving or disproving the drawn-up hypotheses. The entire facets of the study are intricately designed prior to data collection. The tools (questionnaires) were used for the purpose of collecting numerical data. Additionally, quantitative experiments weed out external factors, and in cases where it is properly designed, it normally represents a real and unbiased statement.

RESEARCH INSTRUMENT

A quantitative research methodology is employed where a questionnaire was used as the major research instrument. A questionnaire is a research instrument in which "all techniques of data collection whereby each respondent is asked to respond to the same set of questions in a predetermined order" (De Vaus, 2002, cited in Saunders *et al.*, 2009, p. 360).

The questionnaire used consist of well-established items from the literature, to investigate the level of adaptation by the Malaysian export organizations in their exporting activities. The items used in the questionnaire were adapted from the work of a number of researchers in the field of marketing mix and export adaptation (Jain, 1989; Cavusgil & Zou, 1994; Cavusgil, Zou & Naidu, 1993; Chung, 2002; Shoham, 1999; Park, 2006).

Specifically, the degree of marketing adaptation is a function of a group of antecedent factors, namely international experience, technology intensity, level of competition, government regulation, cultural differences, economic differences, physical conditions, exporting country image and marketing infrastructure (Park, 2006). Items measuring these factors were adapted from a number of research studies in the literature, namely (Cavusgil *et al.*, 1993; CavusgiI & Zou, 1994; Lages & Montgomery, 2001; Chung, 2003; Shoham, 1999; Park, 2006). All these items were measured on a five point Likert-scale in line with the available literature of the previous mentioned studies. Specifically, the items measuring the marketing mix adaptation strategies which include product adaptation, promotion adaptation, distribution adaptation and pricing adaptation, were adopted from Park (2006), who conducted a study to examine the impact of a number of antecedent factors on the export performance of Korean industrial manufacturers. Likewise, the items measuring the marketing mix adaptation strategies were also adapted from Park's (2006) study and were also measured on a five point Likert-scale in line with the available literature of the previous mentioned studies. Finally, the items measuring the construct of export performance was adopted from Albaum and Tse (2001), who conducted a study to examine the impact of a number of antecedent factors on the export performance of Hong Kong exporters. It should be kept in mind that the items were modified as to suit the Malaysian context of the study for example the words Korea/Korean were replaced by Malaysia/Malaysian.

DATA COLLECTION PROCEDURES

The data was collected through the use of a questionnaire distributed among Malaysian firms engaged in exporting activities in the global market. In the study, a Malaysian firm is the unit of analysis (organization); a firm involved in exporting activities internationally. Hence, a questionnaire was distributed among the firms in order to examine the degree of adaptation and their export performance in the foreign markets. The respondents comprised top management of the companies involved in exporting activities, like export managers or general managers as stated on the job title by the firm.

Both types of surveys, namely E-mail survey technique and the self-administered survey technique were utilized. Evidence has compounded the advantages of email surveys in that they are relatively inexpensive to administer and can be easily distributed to a wider audience. In addition, they also provide the respondent with the convenience of filling out the questionnaires in a suitable fashion. However, it also entails various disadvantages; a email survey response rate is normally low, and hence, not the best instrument for a detailed inquiry.

Having completed data collection, random calls were made to some export managers who participated in answering the questionnaires as to ensure that enumerators were accurate in targeting the right respondents. Finally, the nature of the research objectives and the items of the questionnaire were explained in details to the participants before starting answering the questionnaires. The respondents were also encouraged to raise any questions in case any item in the questionnaire is not fully understood.

VARIABLES AND CONSTRUCT

This study involves several variables, namely independent variables, dependent variable and mediating variables. As mentioned in the previous chapter, independent variables include the antecedent factors previously mentioned.

Independent Variables

Independent variables are those variables which are assumed to influence or determine the dependent variable. It is a variable whose value helps pinpoint the value of other variables. It is a variable whose value represents the determination of the modification of the dependent variable. In the study, the antecedent factors represent the independent variables as it was presumed them to influence the dependent variable. These independent variables are as follows:

1. ***International Experience***: The concept of international experience is related to the level of experience acquired by the firm as an international business player (Cavusgil & Zou, 1994). In this context, Terpstra (1987) argues that international experience allows firms to account for dissimilarities between markets and react to the idiosyncrasies of each local market with a modified marketing strategy. In the context of the present research, the construct of international experience was measured on a five-point-Likert Scale, measuring three main criteria. In the first criterion, the respondents were asked to indicate the level of their firm's export experience ranging from none (1) to considerable (5). In the second criterion, the respondents were asked to state the number of the years of export experience their firms have been involved also on a five-point-Likert Scale, that comprised: (1) 1-4 years; (2) 5-9 years; (3) 10-14 years; (4) 15-19 years; and (5) 20 years and above.

2. *Technology Intensity*: A number of researchers argue that technology intensive products, such as computer hardware, aircrafts, semiconductors, photographic equipment, heavy equipment, and machine tools need less adaptation strategies as compared to less technology intensive or traditional products, such as clothing, food, toiletries and household cleaners, because the latter product category is more sensitive and appeals to tastes, customs, and habits of each society (Cavusgil & Zou, 1994). In this context, Jain (1989) argues that if a product meets universal needs of customers, it requires less adaptation. In this study, technology intensity was measured on a five-point-Likert Scale measuring the degree of technology orientation of the industries they are involved in and the measure ranged from not technology intensive (1) to technology intensive (5).

3. *Level of Competition*: An organization needs to modify its marketing strategy when international competition in export markets is present so as to meet the tastes and desires of customers in foreign markets to gain a competitive position over its rivals (Cavusgil, Zou & Naidu, 1993). This would in turn lead to local market expansion and entry into new market segments (Douglas & Craig, 1989). On the other hand, an organization may continuously perform well in foreign markets with a standardized marketing strategy when competition is absent (Jain, 1989). In the present research, the competition level was measured on a five-point-Likert Scale measuring two main criteria. In the first criterion, the respondents were asked to describe the degree of competitive intensity in the main export country on a five-point-Likert Scale ranging from not competitive (1) to very competitive (5). In the second criterion, the respondents were asked to describe the similarity or difference of market share product position between Malaysia and the main export country on a five-point-Likert Scale ranging from very similar (1) to very different (5).

4. *Government Regulation:* Governmental rules, such as product standards, patents, tariffs, non-tariffs, and state participation in business influence all trends of the marketing strategy, thus necessitating an adaptation of marketing program in international markets to suit the rules of the governments of the target markets (Jain, 1989). In this context, Johnson and Arunthanes (1995) observe that differences in legal rules between the home and host market confine the standardization of marketing strategy. In the present research, the construct of government regulation was measured using three main criteria. In the first criterion, respondents were asked to describe the similarity or difference of government regulation on price and sales conditions between Malaysia and the main export country. In the second criterion, the respondents were asked to describe the similarity or difference of government regulation on product content, performance, and safety between Malaysia and the main export country. Finally, in the third criterion, the respondents were asked to describe the similarity or difference of government regulation on packaging requirements between Malaysia and the main export country. All these were measured on a five-point-Likert Scale ranging from very similar (1) to very different (5).

5. *Cultural Differences*: Jeannet and Hennessey (2001: 78) define culture as the "entire heritage of a society transmitted by word or any other form and includes all traditions, habits, religion, art and language". At the international level, it is necessary for marketers to understand culture that influences buyer behavior in foreign markets, which will in turn, formulate the nature of the international marketing policy. Therefore, cultural match between home and foreign markets necessitates the use of a standardized marketing policy (Jain, 1989). In this study, the construct of cultural differences was measured using three main criteria. In the first criterion, respondents were asked to describe the similarity or difference in understanding and interpreting advertisements between Malaysia and the main export country. In the second criterion, the respondents were asked to describe the similarity or difference in consumer literacy and education level between Malaysia and the main export country. Finally, in the third criterion, the respondents were asked to describe the similarity or difference in socio-cultural customs and taboos between Malaysia and the main export country. All these were measured on a five-point-Likert Scale ranging from very similar (1) to very different (5).

6. *Economic Differences*: Differences in the stage of economic and industrial development between national and international markets can have an essential influence on the choice of marketing policy (Park, 2006). In the present research, the construct of economic differences was measured using three main criteria. In the first criterion, respondents were asked to describe the similarity or difference in gross domestic product (GDP) per capital between Malaysia and the main export country. In the second criterion, the respondents were asked to describe the similarity or difference in cost of labor between Malaysia and the main export country. Finally, in the third criterion, the respondents were asked to describe the similarity or difference in stage of economic development between Malaysia and the main export country. All these were measured on a five-point-Likert Scale ranging from very similar (1) to very different (5).

7. *Exporting Country Image:* Albaum, Strandskov and Duerr (2002: 408) argue that country of origin effects is related to the "extent to which the place of manufacture influences product evaluations". In this context, Baalbaki and Malhotra (1993) believe that country of origin affects customer's perception and evaluation of a product. Therefore, the country of origin has a deep influence on the marketing policy and success of a product. In the present research, the construct of exporting country image was measured using three main criteria, by which the image of the Malaysian products in the export countries was assessed. In the first criterion, respondents were asked to state whether the products manufactured by Malaysian firms are perceived as superior to those manufactured by firms in other nations. In the second criterion, the respondents were asked to state whether Malaysia has a good name for producing products, such as the ones produced by their companies. Finally, in the third criterion, the respondents were asked to state whether their reputation is better than competitors' in international markets

8. *Physical Conditions:* Jain (1989) and Shoham (1999) argue that the weather, geography, resources, and size of residential and office buildings are physical conditions of a country. The researchers further elaborate that differences in these physical conditions between the national and international market influence the feasibility of a standardized marketing policy. Furthermore, climate conditions also affect the promotion policy of companies (Jeannet & Hennessey, 2001). In this study, the construct of physical conditions was measured using three main criteria. In the first criterion, respondents were asked to describe the similarity or difference in climate between Malaysia and the main export country. In the second criterion, the respondents were asked to describe the similarity or difference in building density between Malaysia and the main export country. Finally, in the third criterion, the respondents were asked to describe the similarity or difference in residential and office building size between Malaysia and the main export country. All these were measured on a five-point-Likert Scale ranging from very similar (1) to very different (5).

9. *Marketing Infrastructure*: Jain (1989: 75) defines marketing infrastructure as the "institutions and functions necessary to create and develop service demand, including retailers, wholesalers, sales agents, warehousing, transportation, credit, media, and more". The extent of standardization of the marketing strategy is influenced by the accessibility, performance, and cost of the marketing infrastructure in each local market (Jain, 1989). In this study, the final construct on the antecedent factors that influence the marketing mix adaptation, namely the construct of physical conditions was measured using three main criteria. In the first criterion, respondents were asked to describe the similarity or difference in distribution infrastructure between Malaysia and the main export country. In the second criterion, the respondents were asked to describe the similarity or difference in warehousing (e.g., storage warehouse) between Malaysia and the main export country. Finally, in the third criterion, the respondents were asked to describe the similarity or difference in transport (e.g., railroad, water, truck, air) service capability between Malaysia and the main export country. All these were measured on a five-point-Likert Scale ranging from very similar (1) to very different (5).

The following section addresses the measurement of the dependent variable in this study, namely export performance.

In the present research, the antecedent factors that were examined a shaving an influence on the market adaptation strategies, and in turn, the export performance of Malaysian export companies, included nine factors: international experience, technology intensity, level of competition, government regulation, cultural differences, economic differences, physical conditions, exporting country image and marketing infrastructure. The items that measured these factors were adapted from a number of research studies in the literature. All these items were measured on a five-point-Likert Scale in line with the available literature of the previous mentioned studies. The following section addresses the dependent variable of export performance.

Dependent Variable

A dependent variable is the variable measured in the experiment which is being influenced. Normally, the dependent variable reacts to the independent variable, in that it is generally called dependent due to its dependency on the latter. In this study, export performance is considered as dependent variable whereby it is affected by the independent variables comprising antecedent factors, keeping in mind that the effect is done through the mediating variables.

Export Performance

Export performance was measured through the managers' self-evaluation of how their companies are doing as compared to the objectives set by these companies. In this section, the target was to know about the firm's export performance by asking the managers (top management) how they think their companies are doing considering all aspects of the export performance - specifically, to what extent the export performance contributed to the growth, market share, competitiveness and profitability of the firm in the main export country. In other words, managers were asked whether exporting has contributed to the sales growth of the firm, whether exporting has improved their firm's market share, whether export activity has made the firm more competitive, and finally, whether the profitability from the export sales has increased. All these were measured on a five-point-Likert-Scale ranging from strongly disagree (1) to strongly agree (5). These measurements were adapted from Albaum and Tse (2001), who conducted a study to examine the impact of a number of antecedent factors on the export performance of Hong Kong exporters.

Mediating Variable

The mediating variables in this study act as a bridge between the independent variables comprising the factors that were stated earlier and the dependent variable of export performance. In this study, the mediating variables comprise the strategies of adaptation (marketing mix) that are adopted by the Malaysian export organizations.

Marketing Mix

Marketing mix elements comprise a main portion of the firm's export marketing strategy. As mentioned in the previous chapter, prior studies evidenced that export marketing strategy (marketing mix) consists of product, promotion, distribution, and pricing. It is a mediating variable, besides export performance, which also has an affect over the independent variables. Export marketing strategy is measured through four major dimensions, namely product, promotion, distribution and pricing adaptation strategies. The above strategies were evaluated in detail in order to look into the degree of changes or level of adaptation taking place in Malaysian firms, while they export their products internationally. The following section expounds on the operationalization of the four export marketing strategy dimensions.

a) *Product Adaptation*: This study attempts to analyze product adaptation on the basis of their level of adaptation in product quality, product design and style, product features/performance, and product branding. Prior literatures consider these product aspects as the most imperative (Albaum and Tse, 2001; Chung 2003; Özsomer and Simonin, 2004). The firm's entire international experience has some influence on product adaptation, where more extensive product adaptation is customized to local market conditions for the purpose of competing in the host markets (Douglas & Craig, 1989). Experienced firms are inclined to be more attentive and responsive to local market needs and foreign business environment, and are therefore willing to customize their product strategies (Cavusgil, Zou & Naidu, 1993). Product features, namely packaging, services and warranties are changed for the purposes of product adaptation. Additionally, scope as well as export commitment also affect product adaptation strategies through the resources appropriated for the purpose of exporting strategies (Lages & Montgomery, 2004; O'Cass & Julian, 2003). Efforts expanded in changing the product image, product design, color, size and labeling language increase the possibility of product adaptation in the host markets (Ford & Leonidou, 1991; Zou & Stan, 1998; Osman & Ramayah, 2010).

According to Calantone *et al.* (2006), export dependence has been rarely examined as the firm's internal factor although it is one of the factors that are related to export performance through product adaptation strategy. However, evidence of its influence on internal strategies and performance, is few and far between. On the basis of the arguments culled from the resource based theory (Barney, 1991) and industrial theory (Bain, 1968), this study included product adaptation strategy as a firm strategy related to product characteristics, export dependence and openness to innovation, as a firm's internal characteristics (Calantone *et al.*, 2006; Barney, 1991), and industry adaptation and market similarity as external characteristics (Calantone *et al.*, 2006; Bain, 1968). Generally speaking, the firm's level of dependence on exporting positively influences its product adaptation, which means that the greater the dependence, the higher will be the degree of product adaptation strategies. Also, openness to innovation is a feature whereby a firm stimulates its innovation in the marketing activities; an activity imperative to the product adaptation strategy (Bain, 1968; Barney, 1991; Calantone *et al.*, 2006). The willingness and ability of a firm to innovate is affected by absorptive capacity in which the potential capacity can be developed to add to the strategy flexibility, and the ability of the firm to adapt to environmental changes (Cohen & Levinthal, 1990; Zahra & George, 2002).

The degree of adaptation needed by the firms' product strategy is the work of product features, namely product uniqueness, culture-specific products and types of products (Cavusgil, Zou & Naidu, 1993; Cavusgil & Zou, 1994). The differences in the customer needs and conditions require adaptation efforts in product strategy (Douglas & Wind, 1987; Yip, 1997). In addition, economic and industrial differences that exist between home and host markets have a significant influence on the product adaptation strategies (Jain, 1989; Park, 2006). The degree of differences between the economic developments of the markets is found to be positively related to the degree of product adaptation (Chung, 2002). The differences in the consumer purchasing power found in less developed countries and developing countries force firms to modify their products package size and packaging protection (Hill & Still, 1984; Park, 2006). In other words, the higher the differences in the economic development, the greater will be the degree of adaptation needed in the product strategies.

Moreover, government rules and regulations which are permeating the local markets have a great effect on the degree of product adaptation. These government regulations comprise product standards, patents, tariff and non-tariffs insist an adaptation in the product strategies (Cavusgil, Zou & Naidu, 1993; Johnson & Arunthanes, 1995; Truong, 2010). In addition, foreign firms are instructed to conform to government regulations, like measurement units, package size, branding, product performance, technical standards including shape and related attributes, and safety specifications (Boddewyn & Grosse, 1995; Cavusgil, Zou & Naidu, 1993; Johnson & Arunthanes, 1995; Powers & Loyka, 2010). The greater the differences in the government regulations between the home and host markets, the higher will be the product adaptation strategies. Also, cultural differences between the home and host markets affect the degree of adaptation of product strategy, particularly in the consumer goods (Barker & Aydin, 1991; Hill & Still, 1984; Yeung, 2008). Consumer goods like food, drinks, cosmetics, and pharmaceuticals have been found to be greatly sensitive to local cultures and hence, there is that essentiality for firms to change and adapt their product strategy.

(b) *Promotion Adaptation*: Promotion adaptation in this study is analyzed on the basis of the degree the firm adapts its advertising, sales promotion, personal selling and publicity strategies, which are required to customize exports to the local market conditions (Douglas & Craig, 1989). Promotion adaptation is also related to soliciting information in order to enhance promotional strategies for local needs and therefore improving promotional materials and advertisements (Ford & Leonidou, 1991; Zou & Stan, 1998; Osman & Ramayah, 2010). The differences that lie in customer purchasing calls for adaptation of marketing strategies components and hence promotional programs have to be customized accordingly. The level of adaptation of promotional strategy is found to be lower for industrial products compared to consumer goods (Cavusgil, Zou & Naidu, 1993). Promotional practices and promotional budgets have to be modified in foreign firms in order to compete with competitor's offerings, promotion expenditures and their promotional messages (Peebles & Ryans, 1984).

In addition, the level of technology and intensiveness affect the adaptation of promotional strategies. In sum, the more intensive the technology, the lower will be the promotional adaptation (Cavusgil *et al.*, 1993; Cavusgil & Zaou, 1994). Also, adaptation of promotional strategy was revealed to be positively linked to the degree of competition (Cavusgil *et al.*, 1993; Cavusgil & Zou, 1994). In sum, the greater the industry competition, the higher will be the need for firms to adapt their promotional strategy.

Moreover, government regulations influence the aspect of international marketing strategies policy, pushing the firms to take up the promotion adaptation strategy in the foreign market. Also, government regulations regarding the content, message, and timing of advertising, bars firms from adopting standardized advertising campaigns, although they might be more attractive (Jeannet & Hennessey, 2001). The differences in culture between the home and host countries exist as one of the main obstacles in standardized advertising campaigns (Barker & Ayden, 1991). This is because consumers in different countries consider foreign advertisements and campaigns too confusing to comprehend owing to the commercials' reflection of foreign culture, values, lifestyles and unfamiliar atmosphere. Moreover, promotional tools, like sales contests, games and sweepstakes, are not completely acceptable in some cultures because of the social status and symbols it promotes in the society.

(c) *Distribution Adaptation*: In this study, the degree of adaptation in the distribution programs in the local market conditions was analyzed for successful market penetration. According to Douglas and Craig (1989), the distribution strategies of firms should be customized to satisfy the needs of the host markets. This entails recognizing the differences in the business environment between the home and host markets, leading to the modification of distribution strategies (Cavusgil, Zou & Naidu, 1993; Hill & Still, 1984, Mühlbacher *et al.*, 2006). The diverse marketing infrastructures are significant in the distribution adaptation because they influence the distribution process (Ozsomer & Simonin, 2004). In cases where there is a large discrepancy in institutions in the host market, a significant adaptation is needed. Differences in intermediary services, research firms, media and logistical support in host markets require a major adaptation (Jain, 1989; Yip, 1989). Also, differences in the availability, cost and competencies of these institutions from one market to another force firms to adapt to the marketing and distribution strategies (Douglas & Wind, 1987; Harvey, 1993).

In addition differences in the number, size, and dispersion of distributive outlets also force firms to take up a certain levels of adaptation in the distribution strategy (Samiee, 1993). The degree of complexity present in the technology used in the products affects the adaptation of the distribution strategy. The level of complexity of the technology used in the products comprising technical know-how, technical facilities, service support and government regulations, also influence the level of adaptation in the distribution strategies and are significant in modifying the distribution strategies (Cavusgil & Zou, 1994; Jeannet & Hennessey, 2001; Toyne & Walters, 1989). Products that are characterized by high-technology, force firms to modify their distribution strategies towards direct sales approach, while less technology-oriented products can be just distributed through existing retail stores without modification totheir distribution strategy (Jeannet & Hennessey, 2001). In other words, the greater the technology, the greater will be the adaptation of distribution strategies.

The extensiveness of competition existing in the host market can significantly influence the adaptation of distribution strategies. In highly competitive markets, firms are forced to modify and enhance their distribution strategies in order to satisfy market needs. Also, distribution strategies need to be effective and productive in order to set up distribution channels and facilities ahead of competition in host markets (Czinkota & Ronkainen, 1990). In sum, the greater the competition, the higher will be the adaptation required in the distribution strategies. Additionally, economic as well as industrial differences between home and host markets have significant effect on the distribution strategies (Buzzell, 1968; Jain, 1990; Terpstra, 1972). The main function of manufacturers, wholesalers, and retailers significantly differs in developed countries compared to developing countries. These distinctions are positively linked to the degree of adaptation of distribution strategies (Chung, 2002). In sum, the greater the differences in the economic development of the host markets, the higher will be the level of adaptation of distribution strategies needed. The law and regulations surrounding consumer protection may have some effect on the distribution strategy adaptation (Hill & Still, 1984). Government regulations prevent firms from utilizing standardized distribution strategy (Rosenbloom & Larsen, 1991), hence making adaptation a requirement for a successful venture in the foreign market. In sum, the greater the difference in the regulations, the higher will be the degree of adaptation required in the distribution strategy.

In addition, the local culture, comprising customer values, beliefs, attitudes and aesthetic preferences, has a significant influence over the adaptation of distribution strategies (Buzzell, 1968; Hill & Still, 1984). Therefore, it is imperative for the distribution strategies to meet the local cultural norms and preferences represented by shopping habits, location preferences and inventory policies. In sum, the greater the gap in cultures between home and host markets, the greater will be the adaptation needed for distribution strategies.

(d) *Pricing Adaptation*: In this type of adaptation, this study evaluates the degree of adaptation in the firm's pricing strategies across foreign markets. Generally speaking, customer requirements and wants are different from one market to the next; hence, it is vital to keep in mind that the value the customer fixes to the product varies. This requires pricing strategies' adaptation and reflects the price sensitivity of consumers in local markets (Douglas & Wind, 1987; Yip, 1997; Sousa and Bradley, 2008). Marketing adaptation efforts are in play in cases where firms recognize well-structured inter-market segments (Samiee & Roth, 1992). In sum, the greater the difference in the customer needs, the higher will be the degree of adaptation of the pricing strategies.

The differences in marketing infrastructure existing between markets, also have some kind of influence upon the pricing adaptation (Ozsomer & Simonin, 2004). Differences regarding the number, size, distribution outlets, promotional methods, prevailing wholesale and retail margins, price and discount structures, product design and packaging, influence pricing strategies adaptation (Samiee, 1993). In other words, the greater the difference found in the marketing infrastructure, the higher will be the adaptation needed in the pricing strategies.

The complexities surrounding technology-oriented products affect the adaptation of pricing strategies. It has been noted that high technology products often take up a competitive or adaptive pricing strategy for the purpose of widening the demand in the export markets, which is significant in order to for them to recover from the significant technological investment at the onset (Cavusgil & Zou, 1994). Price is found to be positively linked to technology intensiveness, in which case, the greater the technology, the higher will be the price (Jain, 1989).

Moreover, economic and industrial development differences existing between home and host markets have a significant influence upon the pricing adaptation strategies (Buzzell, 1968; Jain, 1989). The economic development of a number of markets confines the acceptable prices for consumers, which leads to obstruction of firms from adopting a standardized pricing strategy (Jain, 1989; Baalbaki & Malhotra, 1993; Jeannet & Heannessey, 2001). Also, the economic environment of the host market revealing the standards of living and employment, income levels, all affect the prices affordable to customers (Jain, 1989).

Additionally, government regulations have some influence on the firm's pricing adaptation strategies. Government regulations comprising antitrust laws, laws regarding dumping and government price controls, force firms to adapt their pricing strategies (Baalbaki & Malhotra, 1993). In addition, regulations covering customer protection also influence pricing (Hill & Still, 1984). In sum, the bigger the difference of government regulations between home and host countries, the higher will be the degree of adaptation of pricing strategies.

Also, the cultural distinctions between home and host markets require the use of pricing adaptation (Johnson & Aruthanes, 1995). According to Cavusgil (1988), national culture of the export markets holds the key to determining the pricing strategy, as in some cultures, high price is linked with high quality; thus, making a standardized pricing strategy across the international markets impossible (Baalbaki & Malhotra, 1993). It is expected that the higher the difference in culture between home and host markets, the greater will be the pricing adaptation strategies.

It is worth mentioning in this context that the four mediating variables, Product Adaptation, Promotion Adaptation, Price Adaptation, and Distribution Adaptation, are also investigated as independent variables, as their impact on export performance was measured. This step was used so as to enrich and further elaborate on the findings of the research. The four adaptation strategies were measured on a five-point-Likert Scale ranging from strongly disagree (1) to strongly agree (5). These measures were adapted from Park (2006) who conducted a study to examine the impact of a number of antecedent factors on the export performance of Korean industrial manufacturers.

POPULATION AND SAMPLING

The population chosen for the current study was Malaysian firms involved in manufacturing and exporting products in foreign markets. The population frame was taken from an authoritative source published by MITI and FMM data directories.

In both databases are listed an excess of more than 3,000 firms; most of these firms are involved in exporting. Therefore, a sample of firms that are indeed involved were identified and listed. The number of firms included in the culled sample represents the real population and sample whereby census sampling was used for the purpose of enhancement and increment of the response level. For the purpose of this study, a population of 3,000 export companies was identified to constitute the population. Drawing from the table provided by Sekaran (2003), the sample size of 341 was recommended. In the current research, a sample of 780 export companies was targeted. The number exceeds the recommended sample and this was done as it was expected that not all the targeted respondents would return all 780 usable questionnaires. In other words, the sample size exceeded the recommended sample size that was proposed by Sekaran (2003), so that a reasonable response rate would be ensured. In addition, the sample of the study was taken randomly and the firms were classified into many sections based on their specialties. However, the number of these firms was not even so 16 per cent of each section following the alphabetical order were selected. The response rate varied from half of the targeted firms or a little more or less. This is due to the idea that some respondents were not interested and others were busy.

Prior to data collection, companies' profiles were gained from different sources but mainly from a number of Malaysian agencies that facilitate export activities and exporting organizations in Malaysia. Having gained the profiles of the companies, that included the companies' locations, exporting activities, contact details and some other related information, the companies were contacted through direct phone calls and emails. It should be kept in mind that not all contact details were listed in the agencies, especially the emails and phone numbers, and that is why the companies' websites were targeted online in which all relevant contact details were listed. All these firms were local firms and attempt was made to exclude any multinational or international companies. This is because these international and multinational companies are not regarded as fully Malaysian companies. Furthermore, these firms export various types of products such as food products, petroleum products, beverages and other types of products. A detailed list of these products could be found in chapter four particularly in Table 4.1.

DATA ANALYSIS

Descriptive and inferential statistics were used to analyze the data for the purpose of examining the degree of adaptation and their effect on firm's export performance. Data collected were analyzed using SPSS version 16.0 for purposes of descriptive statistics on the demographic characteristics of the subjects and exploratory factor analysis, while Partial Least Square (PLS) was used to determine the interactions between the various constructs for ascertaining the various structured equation models. The Beta in the reports was interpreted in terms of the relationship between the variables. The R-square in the reports indicated the amount of variance explained in the dependent variable by the predictors (Cavana, Dlahaye & Sekaran, 2001).

Partial Least Squares (PLS) is a wide class of methods for modeling relations between sets of observed variables by means of latent variables. It comprises of regression and classification tasks as well as dimension reduction techniques and modeling tools. The underlying assumption of all PLS methods is that the observed data is generated by a system or process which is driven by a small number of latent (not directly observed or measured) variables. Projections of the observed data to its latent structure by means of PLS were developed by Herman Wold and coworkers (Wold, 1982; 1985; Wold, Ruhe, Wold & Dunn III, 1984). PLS has received a great amount of attention in the fields of marketing, bioinformatics, food research, medicine, pharmacology, social sciences, physiology–to name but a few. The data collected were analyzed by using the PLS technique, and the results are presented in the next section.

Four
Data Analysis and Findings

INTRODUCTION

The results of the questionnaire conducted are displayed and discussed in this chapter. The data collected are analyzed by using SPSS version 16.0 for purposes of descriptive statistics on the demographic characteristics of the subjects and exploratory factor analysis; PLS was used to determine the interactions between the various constructs. The Beta in the reports was interpreted in terms of the relationship between the variables. The R-square in the reports indicates the amount of variance explained in the dependent variable by the predictors (Cavana *et al.*, 2001).

RESPONSE RATE

From the initial 780 questionnaires that were distributed, the total number of usable responses resulting from this process was 401, representing a response rate of 51.4 per cent. Potential non response bias was assessed by comparing returned questionnaires on key variables (Armstrong and Overton, 1977). No significant differences were found between the early and late respondents (the first 25% of the respondents vs. the last 25% of the respondents) on any of the key variables. We later tested the respondents into three separate groups (33.33% or n = around 134 in each group). Again, we found no significant differences in responses across the three groups. Consequently, it was ensured that non-response bias would not create a major problem.

DESCRIPTIVE STATISTICS

Taking into account that the unit of analysis was the Malaysian export companies, the information related to these companies that was asked in the questionnaires covered the types of products these companies export and also the names of countries these companies export to. Furthermore, the total population of the study was nearly 3,000 export companies in Malaysia. Drawing from the table provided by Sekaran (2003), a recommended sample size would be 341. Keeping in mind that the total number of usable returned questionnaires was 401, this study is believed to be following the right research procedures.

Export Product

In the study, 52 different types of products were reported. Table 4.1 lists the export products by organizations, comprising the total number of 52 types of products.

Table 4.1: List of Export Products by Malaysian exporting organizations

No.	*Organization's Export Products*	*No. of Respondents*	*Percentage (%)*
1.	Beverage	10	2.5%
2.	Local fruits	8	2%
3.	Bird's Nest	4	1%
4.	Tyres	10	2.5%
5.	Palm oil	16	4%
6.	Petroleum	6	1.5%
7.	Woodbed	2	0.5%
8.	Office furniture	2	0.5%
9.	Timber	6	1.5%
10.	Gloves	6	1.5%
11.	Pepper	12	3%
12.	Textiles	10	2.5%
13.	Computer parts	2	0.5%
14.	Plywood	8	2%
15.	Electrical	4	1%
16.	Electronic	4	1%
17.	Rattan	4	1%
18.	Cocoa	6	1.5%
19.	Pineapple	4	1%
20.	Coconut	4	1%
21.	Rubber	2	0.5%
22.	Air conditioners	10	2.5%
23.	Fish – koi	8	2%
24.	Fertilizer	12	3%
25.	Seafood	6	1.5%
26.	Halal food	4	1%
27.	Organic food	2	0.5%
28.	Oil	12	3%
29.	Gas	10	2.5%
30.	Tin	8	2%
31.	Gold	10	2.5%
32.	Silver	8	2%
33.	Glass	8	2%
34.	Rice	10	2.5%
35.	Tea	12	3%
36.	Condoms	12	3%

No.	*Organization's Export Products*	*No. of Respondents*	*Percentage (%)*
37.	Alarm systems	12	3%
38.	Books	14	3.5%
39.	Plastic	10	2.5%
40.	Herbs	14	3.5%
41.	Toys	10	2.5%
42.	Aluminum	8	2%
43.	Bamboo	2	0.5%
44.	Home appliances	2	0.5%
45.	Computers	10	2.5%
46.	Chemicals	10	2.5%
47.	Clothes	2	0.5%
48.	Clay	12	3%
49.	Battery	12	3%
50.	Boats	14	3.5%
51.	Curry powder	4	1%
52.	Tiger prawns	3	0.5%
	Total	**401**	100%

As can be seen in the above Table 4.1, 52 different items appear to be the main products being exported to different countries around the world. The name of the product is written in the first row followed by the number of respondents and the final row represents the percentage of the products.

Export Country

In the study, sixteen countries were reported as export destinations targeted by the Malaysian export organizations. Table 4.2 is a list of the export countries targeted by Malaysian export organizations:

It can be seen from the table above that U.S.A. is the largest export market for Malaysian companies, where the percentage of companies that export to the US was 11.2 per cent, followed by China as a second largest export market for Malaysian companies by 10 per cent. Singapore was the third largest export market for Malaysian companies by a percentage of 9.2 per cent. The lowest percentage was the country of Sri Lanka by a percentage of 0.5 per cent.

To elaborate more on the export countries, five main categories were adopted in this study. Firms that export to 1-2 countries were classified in one group, 3-4 countries into another group, and groups for 5-6 countries, 7-8 countries, and finally, more than 9 countries. The Table 4.3 shows the number of countries that the companies export to according to groups.

From Table 4.3, it can be seen that 29 companies out of the 401 sample companies export to 1-2 countries, eight companies out of the 401 sample companies export to 3-4 countries, 19 companies out of the 401 sample companies export to 5-6 countries, 34 companies out of the 401 sample

Table 4.2: List of Export Countries Targeted by Malaysian Exporting Organizations

	Country	Frequency	Per cent	Valid Per cent	Cumulative Per cent
Valid	Korea	18	4.5	4.5	4.5
	Vietnam	12	3.0	3.0	7.5
	Sri Lanka	2	.5	.5	8.0
	Laos	14	3.5	3.5	11.5
	Thailand	26	6.5	6.5	18.0
	USA	45	11.2	11.2	29.2
	Taiwan	12	3.0	3.0	32.2
	Philippine	23	5.7	5.7	37.9
	Singapore	37	9.2	9.2	47.1
	China	40	10.0	10.0	57.1
	Australia	32	8.0	8.0	65.1
	England	35	8.7	8.7	73.8
	Indonesia	26	6.5	6.5	80.3
	India	20	5.0	5.0	85.3
	Hong Kong	17	4.2	4.2	89.5
	Japan	29	7.2	7.2	96.8
	Myanmar	13	3.2	3.2	100.0
	Total	4011	100.0	100.0	

Table 4.3: The number of Countries Companies Export to

Number of Countries	Frequency	Per cent
1-2 country/ies	29	7.2
3-4 countries	8	2.0
5-6 countries	19	4.7
7-8 countries	34	8.5
9 and more countries	311	77.6
Total	401	100.0

companies export to 7-8 countries, and finally, majority of the companies (311 companies) export to more than 9 countries.

Distribution Channels

In this study, seven main distribution channels were reported. Table 4.4 represents the channels through which the products were distributed by the Malaysian export companies.

The results in Table 4.4 indicate that the direct selling was the most used distributional channel adopted by Malaysian export companies, where the percentage of companies that used direct selling was 28.9 per cent of the total Malaysian export companies, followed by export management company at home with 21.7 per cent of total companies.

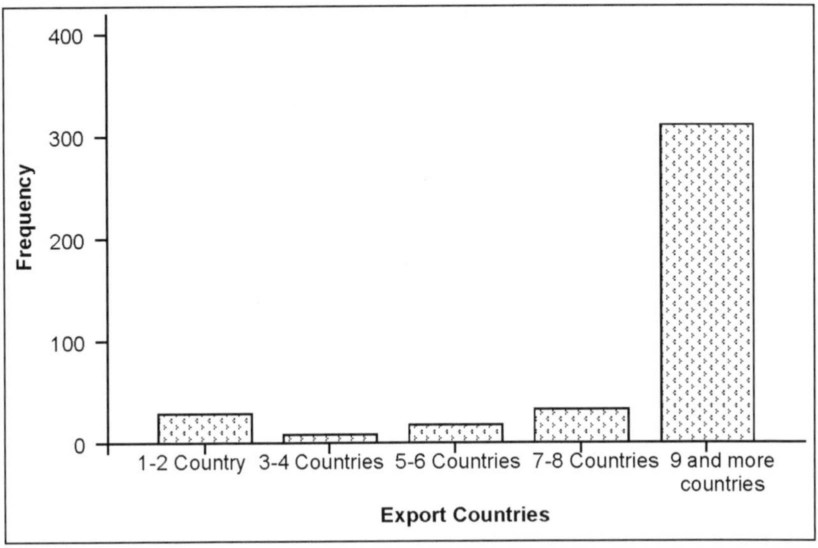

Figure 4.1: Export Countries

Table 4.4: List of Distribution Channels adopted by the Malaysian Export Companies

Channel	*Frequency*	*Per cent*
Independent distributor at target	28	7.0%
Independent agent at target	44	11.0%
Export management company at home	87	21.7%
Trading company at home	62	15.5%
Direct selling	116	28.9%
Joint venture or strategic alliance	26	6.5%
Company owned subsidiary in target	38	9.5%
Total	**401**	**100%**

Export Experience

In this study, the organizations' experience in exporting activities ranged from one to over 20 years of experience. Five main categories of ranges were adopted in this study. Firms that had 1-4 years of experience were classified in one group, 5-9 years in another group, 10-14 years in another group and 15-19 years in another group. Finally, firms that had more than 20 years of experience were classified in another group. Table 4.5 represents range of experiences in exporting activities that Malaysian companies have.

In Table 4.5, it can be seen that 27 companies out of the 401 sample companies had an export experience of 1-4 years, 14 companies out of the 401 sample companies had an export experience of 5-9 years, 15 companies out of the 401 sample companies had an export experience of 10-14 years, and 34 companies out of the 401 sample companies had an export experience

Table 4.5: Export Experience

Range	*Frequency*	*Per cent*
1-4 years	27	6.7
5-9 years	14	3.5
10-14 years	15	3.7
15-19 years	34	8.5
20 years and more	311	77.6
Total	401	100.0

of 15-19 years. Finally, majority of the companies (311 companies) had an export experience of over than 20 years.

INSTRUMENT RELIABILITY AND VALIDITY

Following the two-step approach recommended by Zikmund (2000), adequacy of each multi-item scale in capturing its construct was assessed using the measurement model of all constructs by checking internal consistency reliability, convergent validity and discriminant validity, before testing the hypotheses via the causal model. Several tests were performed on the measurement models to examine their validity and reliability. First, the composite reliability for the internal consistency was demonstrated, since values for all constructs were above the suggested threshold of 0.60 (Fronell and Larcker, 1981) (Table 4.6), and the lowest value of composite reliability was 0.95, which is larger than the recommended value of 0.60, showing good reliability. Convergent validity was assessed by examining Average Variance Extracted (AVE) from the measures. For AVE, a score of 0.5 indicates acceptability (Fornell and Larcker, 1981). From Table 4.6, we can see the AVE ranges from 0.827 to 0.988, which shows convergent validity. Also, the Cronbach's Alpha for all constructs are above 0.70, which implies a high reliability of the measures.

Second, the standardized factor loadings for all items are above the suggested cut-off 0.60 and all are significant, showing strong evidence of convergent validity (Hatcher, 1994). All items are significant with high loadings, which are above the recommended value of 0.60, therefore demonstrating convergent validity.

Table 4.7 presents the discriminant validity statistics. The square roots of the AVE scores (diagonal elements of Table 4.6) are all higher than the correlations among the constructs, thus demonstrating discriminant validity. Cross-loadings of constructs are provided in Table 4.7. All items are loaded higher on their respective constructs than on others, providing additional support for discriminant validity.

Table 4.6: Factor Analysis Results and AVE/CR

Construct	*Items*	*Factor Loading*	*AVE*	*Composite Reliability*	*Cronbachs Alpha*	*R Square*
Export Experience	EXP1	**0.963**				
	EXP2	**0.934**	**0.902**	**0.965**	**0.946**	
	EXP3	**0.952**				
Technology Intensive	TEC1	**NA**	**NA**	**NA**	**NA**	
Competition Level	COM1	**0.980**	**0.959**	**0.979**	**0.957**	
	COM2	**0.979**				
Government Regulations	GOV1	**0.980**				
	GOV2	**0.961**	**0.941**	**0.980**	**0.969**	
	GOV3	**0.970**				
Cultural Differences	CUL1	**0.971**				
	CUL2	**0.972**	**0.939**	**0.979**	**0.968**	
	CUL3	**0.965**				
Economic Differences	ECO1	**0.955**				
	ECO2	**0.940**	**0.892**	**0.961**	**0.940**	
	ECO3	**0.940**				
Company Image	IMG1	**0.985**				
	IMG2	**0.982**	**0.966**	**0.988**	**0.982**	
	IMG3	**0.982**				
Physical Conditions	PHY1	**0.964**				
	PHY2	**0.971**	**0.933**	**0.977**	**0.964**	
	PHY3	**0.963**				
Marketing Infrastructure	INF1	**0.976**				
	INF2	**0.969**	**0.939**	**0.979**	**0.968**	
	INF3	**0.962**				
Product Adaptation	PRD1	**0.957**				
	PRD2	**0.910**	**0.827**	**0.950**	**0.930**	**0.661**
	PRD3	**0.919**				
	PRD4	**0.848**				
Promotion Adaptation	PRM1	**0.950**				
	PRM2	**0.889**	**0.863**	**0.962**	**0.947**	**0.594**
	PRM3	**0.943**				
	PRM4	**0.934**				
Distribution Adaptation	DIS1	**0.940**				
	DIS2	**0.927**	**0.868**	**0.963**	**0.949**	**0.616**
	DIS3	**0.930**				
	DIS4	**0.929**				
Price Adaptation	PRI1	**0.942**				
	PRI2	**0.916**	**0.875**	**0.966**	**0.953**	**0.574**
	PRI3	**0.943**				
	PRI4	**0.942**				
Export Performance	PER1	**0.969**				
	PER2	**0.971**	**0.940**	**0.984**	**0.979**	**0.506**
	PER3	**0.969**				
	PER4	**0.969**				

Table 4.7: Correlations and Average Variance Extracted

	COM	CUL	DIS	ECO	EXP	GOV	IMG	INF	PER	PHY	PRD	PRI	PRM	TEC
COM	**0.98**													
CUL	0.73**	**0.97**												
DIS	0.57**	0.59**	**0.93**											
ECO	0.74**	0.73**	0.67**	**0.94**										
EXP	0.53**	0.40**	0.38**	0.47**	**0.95**									
GOV	0.73**	0.74**	0.60**	0.80**	0.47**	**0.97**								
IMG	0.68**	0.68**	0.60**	0.77**	0.40**	0.72**	**0.98**							
INF	0.65**	0.69**	0.71**	0.73**	0.37**	0.70**	0.68**	**0.97**						
PER	0.45**	0.55**	0.66**	0.54**	0.31**	0.52**	0.54**	0.54**	**0.97**					
PHY	0.71**	0.73**	0.75**	0.78**	0.39**	0.75**	0.71**	0.78**	0.70**	**0.97**				
PRD	0.67**	0.66**	0.67**	0.75**	0.42**	0.72**	0.64**	0.66**	0.60**	0.76**	**0.91**			
PRI	0.61**	0.64**	0.58**	0.65**	0.37**	0.69**	0.60**	0.69**	0.45**	0.64**	0.64**	**0.94**		
PRM	0.61**	0.67**	0.61**	0.66**	0.36**	0.64**	0.59**	0.70**	0.57**	0.72**	0.66**	0.71**	**0.93**	
TEC	0.74**	0.72**	0.57**	0.70**	0.54**	0.77**	0.63**	0.68**	0.51**	0.71**	0.65**	0.61**	0.61**	**1.00**

**. Correlation is significant at the 0.01 level (2-tailed).

In summary, the results of confirmatory factor analysis confirmed the measurement models of which constructs can achieve reliability as well as convergent and discriminate validity. Therefore, it was concluded that the research model is appropriate in terms of goodness of fit.

HYPOTHESES TESTING

By using Smart-PLS, SEM was built that represents the causal relationships among the four variables in this study. SEM was used to assess the relationships among latent variables in the model. It contained the direct and linear paths that combined the latent variables (constructs) with each other. These relationships were considered by seeing structural coefficients on the paths between two constructs respectively (Hien, 2010).

The strong point of the SEM is that it has been one of the most useful multivariate analysis techniques because it is capable of estimating multiple equations simultaneously, measuring latent variables as well as taking measurement error account into the estimation process (Won, 2004). Besides, SEM is a particularly attractive choice when testing mediating variables, in that in SEM, all of the relevant paths are directly tested and complications such as measurement error and feedback, are incorporated directly into the model (Manolova *et al.*, 2008).

RESULTS OF STRUCTURAL MODEL

The structural model results are illustrated in Figure 4.6. Standardized regression weights and t-values are shown in Tables 4.8 to 4.18. Thus, the confirmation results of the proposed hypotheses are as follows:

International Experience Hypotheses Testing

The results of testing the hypotheses of international experience which specifies the relationship between International Experience, as independent variable, and the mediating variable (the marketing mix adaptation) elements are presented in Table 4.8.

Table 4.8: Testing Hypotheses of International Experience

Path	*Effect*	*Path Coefficient*	*t Statistics*	*Result*
EXP -> PRD	Direct	0.030	1.393	Not Significant
EXP -> PRM	Direct	0.026	0.920	Not Significant
EXP -> DIS	Direct	0.088	2.769**	Significant
EXP -> PRI	Direct	0.008	0.382	Not Significant

*** $p < .001$, ** $p < .01$, * $p < .05$, based on two-tailed test; $t\ (p < .001) = 3.29$; $t\ (p < .01) = 2.58$; $t\ (p < .05) = 1.96$.

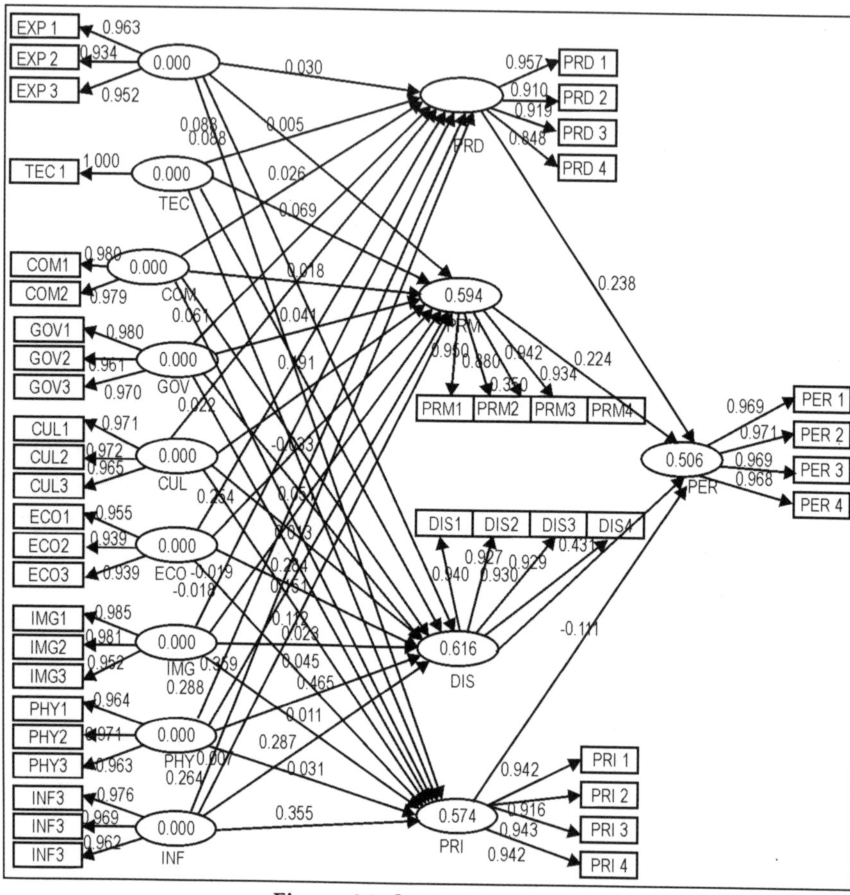

Figure 4.2: Structural Model

Hypothesis 1: The greater the international experience, the greater the likelihood that Malaysian exporters will adapt their marketing mix strategy.

H1a: specifies that the greater the international experience, the greater the likelihood that Malaysian exporters will adapt their product strategy. This hypothesis was not verified (with the path coefficient = 0.030; t = 1.393). This shows that there is no relationship between company's experience in the export business and its product strategy adaptation. As a result, H1a is not significant.

In this study international experience refers to the number of years Malaysian companies gained from exporting their products to other countries. This result indicates that there is no significant effect of international experience on product strategy of Malaysian export companies.

H1b: specifies that the greater the international experience, the greater the likelihood that Malaysian exporters will adapt their promotion strategy.

This hypothesis was not verified (with the path coefficient = 0.026; t = 0.920). This shows that the there is no relationship between company's experience in the export business and its promotion strategy adaptation. As a result, H1b is not significant.

H1c: specifies that the greater the international experience, the greater the likelihood that Malaysian exporters will adapt their distribution strategy. This hypothesis was verified (with the path coefficient = 0.088; t = 2.769). This shows that the greater the company's experience in the export business, the greater the level of its distribution strategy adaptation in export markets. As a result, H1c is significant.

H1d: specifies that the greater the international experience, the greater the likelihood that Malaysian exporters will adapt their pricing strategy. This hypothesis was not verified (with the path coefficient = 0.008; t = 0.382). It shows that the there is no relationship between company's experience in the export business and its pricing strategy adaptation. As a result, H1d is not significant.

Technology Intensity Hypotheses Testing

The results of testing the hypotheses of technology intensity which specifies the relationship between technology intensity, as independent variable, and the dependent variable (the marketing mix adaptation) elements are presented in Table 4.9.

Table 4.9: Testing Hypotheses of Technology Intensity

Path	*Effect*	*Path Coefficient*	*t Statistics*	*Result*
TEC -> PER	Indirect	–0.021	0.488	Not Significant
TEC -> PRD	Direct	0.005	0.083	Not Significant
TEC -> PRM	Direct	0.001	0.023	Not Significant
TEC -> DIS	Direct	–0.049	0.638	Not Significant
TEC -> PRI	Direct	0.007	0.103	Not Significant

*** $p < .001$, ** $p < .01$, * $p < .05$, based on two-tailed test; $t\ (p < .001) = 3.29$; $t\ (p < .01) = 2.58$; $t\ (p < .05) = 1.96$.

Hypothesis 2: The greater the technology intensity, the greater the likelihood that Malaysian exporters will adapt their marketing mix strategy.

Technology intensity refers to how technological oriented the products exported by Malaysian companies to other countries are.

H2a: specifies that technology intensity of the industry is positively associated with the degree of product adaptation of Malaysian exporters. This hypothesis was not verified (with the path coefficient = 0.005; t = 0.083). This shows that there is no relationship between the technology intensity of the industry and its product strategy adaptation. As a result, H2 is not significant.

H2b: specifies that technology intensity is negatively associated with the degree of promotion adaptation of Malaysian exporters. This hypothesis was not verified (with the path coefficient = 0.001; t = 0.023). This shows that here is no relationship between the technology intensity of the industry and its promotion strategy adaptation. As a result, H2b is not significant.

H2c: specifies that technology intensity is negatively associated with the degree of distribution adaptation of Malaysian exporters. This hypothesis was not verified (with the path coefficient = –0.049; t = 0.638). This shows that the there is no relationship between the technology intensity of the industry and its distribution strategy adaptation. As a result, H2c is not significant.

H2d: specifies that technology intensity is positively associated with the degree of pricing adaptation of Malaysian exporters. This hypothesis was not verified (with the path coefficient = 0.007; t = 0.103). This shows that there is no relationship between the technology intensity of the industry and its pricing strategy adaptation. As a result, H2d is not significant.

Competition Level Hypotheses Testing

Competition level refers to how competitive the market in the host countries is. The results of testing the hypotheses of competition level which specifies the relationship between competition level, as independent variable, and the dependent variable (the marketing mix adaptation) elements are presented in Table 4.10.

Table 4.10: Testing Hypotheses of Competition Level

Path	*Effect*	*Path Coefficient*	*T Statistics*	*Result*
COM -> PRD	Direct	0.070	0.828	Not Significant
COM -> PRM	Direct	0.018	0.328	Not Significant
COM -> DIS	Direct	–0.033	0.448	Not Significant
COM -> PRI	Direct	0.061	0.916	Not Significant

*** $p < .001$, ** $p < .01$, * $p < .05$, based on two-tailed test; $t\ (p < .001) = 3.29$; $t\ (p < .01) = 2.58$; $t\ (p < .05) = 1.96$.

Hypothesis 3: The greater the competition level of the industry, the greater the likelihood that Malaysian exporters will adapt their marketing mix strategy.

H3a: specifies that the competition level of the industry is related to the degree of product adaptation of Malaysian exporters. This hypothesis was not verified (with the path coefficient = 0.070; t = 0.0828). This shows that there is no relationship between the competition level of the industry and its product strategy adaptation. As a result, H3a is not significant.

H3b: specifies that the competition level of the industry is related to the degree of promotion adaptation of Malaysian exporters. This hypothesis was not verified (with the path coefficient = 0.018; t = 0.328). This shows that there is no relationship between the competition level of the industry and its promotion strategy adaptation. As a result, H3b is not significant.

H3c: specifies that the competition level of the industry is related to the degree of distribution adaptation of Malaysian exporters. This hypothesis was not verified (with the path coefficient = –0.033; t = 0.448). This shows that there is no relationship between the competition level of the industry and its distribution strategy adaptation. As a result, H3c is not significant.

H3d: specifies that the competition level of the industry is related to the degree of pricing adaptation of Malaysian exporters. This hypothesis was not verified (with the path coefficient = 0.061; t = 0.917). This shows that there is no relationship between the competition level of the industry and its pricing strategy adaptation. As a result, H3d is not significant.

Government Regulations Hypotheses Testing

Government regulations refer to the rules and regulations that are set by the host countries. The results of testing the hypotheses of government regulations which specifies the relationship between government regulations, as independent variable, and the dependent variable (the marketing mix adaptation) elements are presented in Table 4.11.

Table 4.11: Testing Hypotheses of Government Regulations

Path	*Effect*	*Path Coefficient*	*T Statistics*	*Result*
GOV -> PRD	Direct	0.169	2.263*	Significant
GOV -> PRM	Direct	0.041	0.645	Not Significant
GOV -> DIS	Direct	–0.051	0.716	Not Significant
GOV -> PRI	Direct	0.284	3.499***	Significant

*** $p < .001$, ** $p < .01$, * $p < .05$, based on two-tailed test; t ($p < .001$) = 3.29; t ($p < .01$) = 2.58; t ($p < .05$) = 1.96.

Hypothesis 4: The greater the difference of government regulations, the greater the likelihood that Malaysian exporters will adapt their marketing mix strategy.

H4a: specifies that the greater the difference of government regulations between home and export market, the greater the likelihood that Malaysian exporters will adapt their product strategy. This hypothesis was verified (with the path coefficient = 0.169; t = 2.263). This shows that the difference of government regulations between home and export market will lead Malaysian export companies to adapt their product strategy. As a result, H4a is significant.

H4b: specifies that the greater the difference of government regulations between home and export market, the greater the likelihood that Malaysian exporters will adapt their promotion strategy. This hypothesis was not verified (with the path coefficient = 0.041; t = 0.645). This shows that there is no relationship between the difference of government regulations between home and export market and its promotion strategy adaptation. As a result, H4b is not significant.

H4c: specifies that the greater the difference of government regulations between home and export market, the greater the likelihood that Malaysian exporters will adapt their distribution strategy. This hypothesis was not verified (with the path coefficient = –0.0511; t = 0.716). This shows that there is no relationship between the difference of government regulations between home and export market and its distribution strategy adaptation. As a result, H4c is not significant.

H4d: specifies that the greater the difference of government regulations between home and export market, the greater the likelihood that Malaysian exporters will adapt their pricing strategy. This hypothesis was verified (with the path coefficient = 0.248; t = 3.499). This shows that there is a relationship between the difference of government regulations between home and export market and its pricing strategy adaptation. As a result, H4d is significant.

Cultural Differences Hypotheses Testing

Cultural difference refers to the differences in the cultural aspects between Malaysia and the host countries. These cultural aspects include language, religion, heritage and lifestyles. The results of testing the hypotheses of cultural differences which specify the relationship between cultural differences, as independent variable, and the dependent variable (the marketing mix adaptation) elements are presented in Table 4.12.

Table 4.12: Testing Hypotheses of Cultural Differences

Path	Effect	Path Coefficient	T Statistics	Result
CUL -> PRD	Direct	0.022	0.339	Not Significant
CUL -> PRM	Direct	0.191	2.246*	Significant
CUL -> DIS	Direct	–0.013	0.193	Not Significant
CUL -> PRI	Direct	0.112	1.120	Not Significant

*** $p < .001$, ** $p < .01$, * $p < .05$, based on two-tailed test; t ($p < .001$) = 3.29; t ($p < .01$) = 2.58; t ($p < .05$) = 1.96.

Hypothesis 5: The greater the cultural differences between Malaysia and export market, the greater the likelihood that Malaysian exporters will adapt their marketing mix strategy.

H5a: specifies that the greater the cultural differences between Malaysia and export market, the greater the degree of product strategy adaptation of Malaysian exporters. This hypothesis was not verified (with the path coefficient = 0.022; t = 0.339). This shows that the cultural differences between Malaysia and export market will not affect Malaysian export companies to adapt their product strategy. As a result, H5a is not significant.

H5b: specifies that the greater the cultural differences between Malaysia and export market, the greater the degree of promotion strategy adaptation of Malaysian exporters. This hypothesis was verified (with the path coefficient = 0.191; t = 2.246). This shows that the cultural differences between home and export market will lead Malaysian export companies to adapt their promotion strategy. As a result, H5b is significant.

H5c: specifies that the greater the cultural differences between Malaysia and export market, the greater the degree of distribution strategy adaptation of Malaysian exporters. This hypothesis was not verified (with the path coefficient = –.013; t = 0.193). This shows that the cultural differences between Malaysia and export market will not affect Malaysian export companies to adapt their distribution strategy. As a result, H5c is not significant.

H5d: specifies that the greater the cultural differences between Malaysia and export market, the greater the degree of pricing strategy adaptation of Malaysian exporters. This hypothesis was not verified (with the path coefficient = 0.112; t = 1.120). This shows that the cultural differences between Malaysia and export market will not affect Malaysian export companies to adapt their pricing strategy. As a result, H5d is not significant.

Economic Differences Hypotheses Testing

Economic difference refers to the economical differences between Malaysia and the host countries which includes rate exchange and economy of scale and the difference in the purchase power or the ability of people to buy products depending on their economical status. The results of testing the hypotheses of economic differences which specifies the relationship between economic differences, as independent variable, and the dependent variable (the marketing mix adaptation) elements are presented in Table 4.13.

Table 4.13: Testing Hypotheses of Economic Differences

Path	*Effect*	*Path Coefficient (PC)*	*T Statistics (|PC/SE|)*	*Result*
ECO -> PRD	Direct	0.254	2.791**	Significant
ECO -> PRM	Direct	0.071	0.569	Not Significant
ECO -> DIS	Direct	0.151	1.631	Not Significant
ECO -> PRI	Direct	0.045	0.619	Not Significant

*** $p < .001$, ** $p < .01$, * $p < .05$, based on two-tailed test; t ($p < .001$) = 3.29; t ($p < .01$) = 2.58; t ($p < .05$) = 1.96.

Hypothesis 6: The greater the economic differences between the exporters' home market and foreign markets, the greater the likelihood that Malaysian exporters will adapt their marketing mix strategy.

H6a: specifies that the greater the economic differences between the exporters' home market and foreign market, the greater the level of adaptation of product strategy of Malaysian exporters. This hypothesis was verified (with the path coefficient = 0.254; t = 2.791). This shows that the economic differences between exporters' home market and foreign market will lead the export companies to adapt their products to suit these differences. As a result, H6a is significant.

H6b: specifies that the greater the economic differences between the exporters' home market and foreign market, the greater the level of adaptation of promotion strategy of Malaysian exporters. This hypothesis was not verified (with the path coefficient = 0.071; t = 0.569). This shows that the economic differences between Malaysia and export market will not affect Malaysian export companies in level of adaptation of promotion strategy. As a result, H6b is not significant.

H6c: specifies that the greater the economic differences between the exporters' home market and foreign market, the greater the level of adaptation of distribution strategy of Malaysian exporters. This hypothesis was not verified (with the path coefficient = 0.151; t = 1.631). This shows that the economic differences between Malaysia and export market will not affect Malaysian export companies to adapt their distribution strategy. As a result, H6c is not significant.

H6d: specifies that the greater the economic differences between the exporters' home market and foreign market, the greater the level of adaptation of pricing strategy of Malaysian exporters. This hypothesis was not verified (with the path coefficient = 0.045; t = 0.619). This shows that the economic differences between Malaysia and export market will not affect Malaysian export companies to adapt their pricing strategy. As a result, H6d is not significant.

Country Image Hypotheses Testing

Country image refers to how other countries perceive the Malaysian products to be in terms of quality and image. The results of testing the hypotheses of country image which specifies the relationship between country image, as independent variable, and the dependent variable (the marketing mix adaptation) elements are presented in Table 4.14.

Hypothesis7: The greater the negative image of the exporting country (Malaysia), the greater the likelihood that Malaysian exporters will adapt their marketing mix strategy.

H7a: specifies that the greater the negative image of the exporting country (Malaysia), the greater the likelihood that Malaysian exporters will adapt their product strategy to foreign markets. This hypothesis was not verified (with

Table 4.14: Testing Hypotheses of Country Image

Path	*Effect*	*Path Coefficient*	*T Statistics*	*Result*
IMG -> PRD	Direct	–0.010	0.137	Not Significant
IMG -> PRM	Direct	–0.017	0.210	Not Significant
IMG -> DIS	Direct	0.023	0.393	Not Significant
IMG -> PRI	Direct	0.011	0.137	Not Significant

*** $p < .001$, ** $p < .01$, * $p < .05$, based on two-tailed test; $t\ (p < .001) = 3.29$; $t\ (p < .01) = 2.58$; $t\ (p < .05) = 1.96$.

the path coefficient = –0.010; $t = 0.137$). This shows that the negative image of the exporting country (Malaysia) will not affect Malaysian export companies to adapt their product strategy. As a result, H7a is not significant.

H7b: specifies that the greater the negative image of the exporting country (Malaysia), the greater the likelihood that Malaysian exporters will adapt their promotion strategy to foreign markets. This hypothesis was not verified (with the path coefficient = –0.017; $t = 0.210$). This shows that the negative image of the exporting country (Malaysia) will not affect Malaysian export companies to adapt their promotion strategy. As a result, H7b is not significant.

H7c: specifies that the greater the negative image of the exporting country (Malaysia), the greater the likelihood that Malaysian exporters will adapt their distribution strategy to foreign markets. This hypothesis was not verified (with the path coefficient = 0.023; $t = 0.393$). This shows that the negative image of the exporting country (Malaysia) will not affect Malaysian export companies to adapt their distribution strategy. As a result, H7c is not significant.

H7d: specifies that the greater the negative image of the exporting country (Malaysia), the greater the likelihood that Malaysian exporters adapt their pricing strategy to foreign markets. This hypothesis was not verified (with the path coefficient = 0.011; $t = 0.137$). This shows that the negative image of the exporting country (Malaysia) will not affect Malaysian export companies to adapt their pricing strategy. As a result, H7d is not significant.

Physical Conditions Hypotheses Testing

Physical conditions refer to the difference between Malaysia and host countries in terms of weather and climate changes. The results of testing the hypotheses of physical conditions which specifies the relationship between physical conditions, as independent variable, and the dependent variable (the marketing mix adaptation) elements are presented in Table 4.15.

Hypothesis 8: The greater the difference in physical conditions between the local and foreign market, the greater the likelihood that Malaysian exporters will adapt their marketing mix strategy.

H8a: specifies that the greater the difference in physical conditions between the local and foreign market, the greater the likelihood that Malaysian

Table 4.15: Testing Hypotheses of Physical Conditions

Path	*Effect*	*Path Coefficient*	*T Statistics*	*Result*
PHY -> PRD	Direct	0.358	3.879***	Significant
PHY -> PRM	Direct	0.284	3.457***	Significant
PHY -> DIS	Direct	0.465	4.672***	Significant
PHY -> PRI	Direct	–0.031	0.488	Not Significant

*** $p < .001$, ** $p < .01$, * $p < .05$, based on two-tailed test; $t\ (p < .001) = 3.29$; $t\ (p < .01) = 2.58$; $t\ (p < .05) = 1.96$.

exporters will adapt their product strategy in foreign markets. This hypothesis was verified (with the path coefficient = 0.358; $t = 3.879$). This shows that the differences in physical conditions between exporters' home market and foreign market will lead the export companies to adapt their products to suit these differences. As a result, H8a is significant.

H8b: specifies that the greater the difference in physical conditions between the local and foreign market, the greater the likelihood that Malaysian exporters will adapt their promotion strategy in foreign markets. This hypothesis was verified (with the path coefficient = 0.284; $t = 3.457$). This shows that the differences in physical conditions between exporters' home market and foreign market will lead the export companies to adapt their promotion strategy to suit these differences. As a result, H8b is significant.

H8c: specifies that the greater the difference in physical conditions between the local and foreign market, the greater the likelihood that Malaysian exporters will adapt their distribution strategy in foreign markets. This hypothesis was verified (with the path coefficient = 0.465; $t = 4.672$). This shows that the differences in physical conditions between exporters' home market and foreign market will lead the export companies to adapt their distribution strategy to suit these differences. As a result, H8c is significant.

H8d: specifies that the greater the difference in physical conditions between the local and foreign market, the greater the likelihood that Malaysian exporters will adapt their pricing strategy in foreign markets. This hypothesis was not verified (with the path coefficient = –0.031; $t = 0.488$). This shows that the differences in physical conditions between exporters' home market and foreign market will not affect Malaysian export companies to adapt their pricing strategy. As a result, H8d is not significant.

Marketing Infrastructure Hypotheses Testing

Marketing infrastructure refers to the nature and condition of the infrastructure available in the host countries. The results of testing the hypotheses of marketing infrastructure which specifies the relationship between marketing infrastructure, as independent variable, and the dependent variable (the marketing mix adaptation) elements are presented in Table 4.16.

Table 4.16: Testing Hypotheses of Marketing Infrastructure

<SOURCE_1>	*Effect*	*Path Coefficient*	*T Statistics*	*Result*
INF -> PRD	Direct	0.007	0.106	Not Significant
INF -> PRM	Direct	0.254	3.943***	Significant
INF -> DIS	Direct	0.287	3.798***	Significant
INF -> PRI	Direct	0.355	3.983***	Significant

*** $p < .001$, ** $p < .01$, * $p < .05$, based on two-tailed test; t $(p < .001) = 3.29$; t $(p < .01) = 2.58$; t $(p < .05) = 1.96$.

Hypothesis 9: The greater the difference between the marketing infrastructure of the exporters' local and foreign market, the greater the likelihood that Malaysian exporters will adapt their marketing mix strategy.

H9a: specifies that the greater the difference between the marketing infrastructure of the exporters' home market and foreign market, the greater the level of adaptation of the product strategy of Malaysian exporters. This hypothesis was not verified (with the path coefficient = 0.007; t = 0.106). This shows that the differences in marketing infrastructure between exporters' home market and foreign market will not affect Malaysian export companies to adapt their product strategy. As a result, H9a is not significant.

H9b: specifies that the greater the difference between the marketing infrastructure of the exporters' home market and foreign market, the greater the level of adaptation of the promotion strategy of Malaysian exporters. This hypothesis was verified (with the path coefficient = 0.254; t = 3.943). This shows that the differences in marketing infrastructure between exporters' home market and foreign market will lead the export companies to adapt their promotion strategy to suit these differences. As a result, H9b is significant.

H9c: specifies that the greater the difference between the marketing infrastructure of the exporters' home market and foreign market, the greater the level of adaptation of the distribution strategy of Malaysian exporters. This hypothesis was verified (with the path coefficient = 0.287; t = 3.798). This shows that the differences in marketing infrastructure between exporters' home market and foreign market will lead the export companies to adapt their distribution strategy to suit these differences. As a result, H9b is significant.

H9d: specifies that the greater the difference between the marketing infrastructure of the exporters' home market and foreign market, the greater the level of adaptation of the pricing strategy of Malaysian exporters. This hypothesis was verified (with the path coefficient = 0.355; t = 3.983). This shows that the differences in marketing infrastructure between exporters' home market and foreign market will lead the export companies to adapt their pricing strategy to suit these differences. As a result, H9d is significant.

Table 4.17: The impact of antecedent factors on the performance of Malaysian export companies through the mediating influence of marketing mix adaptation

Path	*Effect*	*Path Coefficient*	*T. Statistics*	*Result*
EXP -> PER	Indirect	0.050	2.598**	Significant
TEC -> PER	Indirect	–0.021	0.488	Not Significant
COM -> PER	Indirect	–0.001	0.014	Not Significant
GOV -> PER	Indirect	–0.004	0.101	Not Significant
CUL -> PER	Indirect	0.030	0.756	Not Significant
ECO -> PER	Indirect	0.137	2.421*	Significant
IMG -> PER	Indirect	0.002	0.072	Not Significant
PHY -> PER	Indirect	0.353	5.236***	Significant
INF -> PER	Indirect	0.143	2.790**	Significant

Hypothesis 10: The firm's marketing mix mediates the relationship between the firm's antecedents and the performance of Malaysian export companies.

H10.1: specifies that the marketing mix adaptation mediates the effect of international experience on the performance of Malaysian export companies. This hypothesis was verified (with the path coefficient = 0.050; t = 2.598). This shows that the marketing mix adaptation has an effect on the relationship between company's experiences in the export business and the level of Malaysian export companies' performance in export markets. As a result, H1 is significant.

H10.2: specifies that the marketing mix adaptation mediates the effect of technology intensity on the performance of Malaysian export companies. This hypothesis was not verified (with the path coefficient = –0.021; t = 0.488). This shows that the marketing mix adaptation has no effect on the relationship between technology intensity and the level of Malaysian export companies' performance in export markets. As a result, H2 is not significant.

This result indicates that there is no significant effect of technology intensity on performance of Malaysian export companies. This means that the increased level of technology intensity in the Malaysian market will not affect the performance of Malaysian export companies through the mediating impact of marketing mix strategies.

H10.3: specifies that the marketing mix adaptation mediates the effect of differences of competition between home and export market on performance of Malaysian export companies. This hypothesis was not verified (with the path coefficient = –0.001; t = 0.014). This shows that the marketing mix adaptation has no effect on the relationship between differences of competition between home and export market and the level of Malaysian export companies' performance in export markets. As a result, H3 is not significant.

This result indicates that there is no significant effect of competition level on performance of Malaysian export companies. This means that differences of competition between home and export market will not affect the performance of Malaysian export companies through the mediating impact of marketing mix strategies.

H10.4: specifies that the marketing mix adaptation mediates the effect of differences of government regulations between home and export market on performance of Malaysian export companies. This hypothesis was not verified (with the path coefficient = –0.004; t = 0.101). This shows that the marketing mix adaptation has no effect on the relationship between differences of government regulations between home and export market and the level of Malaysian export companies' performance in export markets. As a result, H4 is not significant.

This result indicates that there is no significant difference of government regulations between home and export market in performance of Malaysian export companies. This means that government regulations between home and export market will not affect the performance of Malaysian export companies through the mediating impact of marketing mix strategies.

H10.5: specifies that the marketing mix adaptation mediates the effect of cultural differences between Malaysia and export market on performance of Malaysian export companies. This hypothesis was not verified (with the path coefficient = 0.030; t = 0.756). This shows that the marketing mix adaptation has no effect on the relationship between cultural differences between Malaysia and export market and the level of Malaysian export companies' performance in export markets. As a result, H5 is not significant.

This result indicates that there is no significant effect of cultural differences on performance of Malaysian export companies. This means that cultural differences between Malaysia and export market will not affect the performance of Malaysian export companies through the mediating impact of marketing mix strategies.

H10.6: specifies that the marketing mix adaptation mediates the effect of economic differences between the exporters' home market and foreign market on performance of Malaysian export companies. This hypothesis was verified (with the path coefficient = 0.137; t = 2.421). This shows that the marketing mix adaptation has an effect on the relationship between economic differences between the exporters' home market and foreign market and the level of Malaysian export companies' performance in export markets. As a result, H6 is significant.

This result indicates that there is a significant difference between the exporters' home market and foreign market in performance of Malaysian export companies. This means that economic differences between the exporters' home market and foreign market will affect the performance of Malaysian export companies, keeping in mind that this effect was done through the mediating impact of marketing mix strategies.

H10.7: specifies that the marketing mix adaptation mediates the effect of the negative image of the exporting country (Malaysia) on performance of Malaysian export companies. This hypothesis was not verified (with the path coefficient = 0.002; t = 0.072). This shows that the marketing mix adaptation has no effect on the relationship between the negative image of the exporting country (Malaysia) and the level of Malaysian export companies' performance in export markets. As a result, H7 is not significant.

This result indicates that there is no significant difference between the negative image of the exporting country (Malaysia) and the performance of Malaysian export companies. This means that the negative image of the exporting country (Malaysia) will not affect the performance of Malaysian export companies, through the mediating impact of marketing mix strategies.

H10.8: specifies that the marketing mix adaptation mediates the effect of differences in physical conditions between the exporters' home market and foreign market on performance of Malaysian export companies. This hypothesis was verified (with the path coefficient = 0.353; t = 5.236). This shows that the marketing mix adaptation has an effect on the relationship between differences in physical conditions between the exporters' home market and foreign market and the level of Malaysian export companies' performance in export markets. As a result, H8 is significant.

This result indicates that there is significant relationship between the differences in physical conditions between the exporters' home market and foreign market and the performance of Malaysian export companies. This means that the differences in physical conditions between the exporters' home market and foreign market will affect the performance of Malaysian export companies, keeping in mind that this effect was done through the mediating impact of marketing mix strategies.

H10.9: specifies that the marketing mix adaptation mediates the effect of differences in marketing infrastructure between the exporters' home market and foreign market on performance of Malaysian export companies. This hypothesis was verified (with the path coefficient = 0.143; t = 2.79). This shows that the marketing mix adaptation has an effect on the relationship between differences in marketing infrastructure between the exporters' home market and foreign market and the level of Malaysian export companies' performance in export markets. As a result, H9 is significant.

This result indicates that there is a significant relationship between differences in marketing infrastructure and the exporters' home market and foreign market and foreign market performance of Malaysian export companies. This means that differences in marketing infrastructure between the exporters' home market and foreign market will affect the performance of

Malaysian export companies, keeping in mind that this effect was done through the mediating impact of marketing mix strategies.

Marketing Mix Hypotheses Testing

The results of testing the hypotheses of marketing mix which specifies the relationship between marketing mix, as independent variable, and the dependent variables (export performance) are presented in Table 4.18.

Table 4.18: Testing Hypotheses of Marketing Mix

Path	*Effect*	*Path Coefficient*	*T Statistics*	*Result*
PRD -> PER	Direct	0.238	3.172**	Significant
PRM -> PER	Direct	0.224	2.971**	Significant
DIS -> PER	Direct	0.431	5.583***	Significant
PRI -> PER	Direct	–0.111	1.937	Not Significant

*** $p < .001$, ** $p < .01$, * $p < .05$, based on two-tailed test; $t\ (p < .001) = 3.29$; $t\ (p < .01) = 2.58$; $t\ (p < .05) = 1.96$.

Hypothesis 11: The greater the firm's level of marketing mix strategy adaptation, the better the Malaysian exporters' performance.

H11a: It specifies that the greater the level of product strategy adaptation, the better the Malaysian exporters' performance. This hypothesis was verified (with the path coefficient = 0.238; t = 3.172). This shows that the product strategy adaptation of Malaysian companies will affect Malaysian export companies' performance. As a result, H10 is significant.

H11b: specifies that the greater the level of promotion strategy adaptation, the better the Malaysian exporters' performance. This hypothesis was verified (with the path coefficient = 0.224; t = 2.971). This shows that the promotion strategy adaptation of Malaysian companies will affect Malaysian export companies' performance. As a result, H11 is significant.

H11c: specifies that the greater the level of distribution strategy adaptation, the better the Malaysian exporters' performance. This hypothesis was verified (with the path coefficient = 0.431; t = 5.583). This shows that the distribution strategy adaptation of Malaysian companies will affect Malaysian export companies' performance. As a result, H12 is significant.

H11d: specifies that the greater the level of pricing strategy adaptation, the better the Malaysian exporters' performance. This hypothesis was not verified (with the path coefficient = –0.111; t = 1.937). This shows that the pricing strategy adaptation of Malaysian companies will not affect Malaysian export companies' performance. As a result, H13 is not significant.

Table 4.19: Research Hypotheses Testing Results

No	Hypothesis	Result
H1a	The greater the international experience, the greater the likelihood that Malaysian exporters will adapt their product strategy.	Not Significant
H1b	The greater the international experience, the greater the likelihood that Malaysian exporters will adapt their promotion strategy.	Not Significant
H1c	The greater the international experience, the greater the likelihood that Malaysian exporters will adapt their distribution strategy.	Significant
H1d	The greater the international experience, the greater the likelihood that Malaysian exporters will adapt their pricing strategy.	Not Significant
H2a	The technology intensity of the industry is positively associated with the degree of product adaptation of Malaysian exporters.	Not Significant
H2b	The technology intensity is negatively associated with the degree of promotion adaptation of Malaysian exporters.	Not Significant
H2c	The technology intensity is negatively associated with the degree of distribution adaptation of Malaysian exporters.	Not Significant
H2d	The technology intensity is positively associated with the degree of pricing adaptation of Malaysian exporters.	Not Significant
H3a	The competition level of the industry is related to the degree of product adaptation of Malaysian exporters.	Not Significant
H3b	The competition level of the industry is related to the degree of promotion adaptation of Malaysian exporters.	Not Significant
H3c	The competition level of the industry is related to the degree of distribution adaptation of Malaysian exporters.	Not Significant
H3d	The competition level of the industry is related to the degree of price adaptation of Malaysian exporters.	Not Significant
H4a	The greater the difference of government regulations between home and export market, the greater the likelihood that Malaysian exporters will adapt their product strategy.	Significant
H4b	The greater the difference of government regulations between home and export market, the greater the likelihood that Malaysian exporters will adapt their promotion strategy.	Not Significant
H4c	The greater the difference of government regulations between home and export market, the greater the likelihood that Malaysian exporters will adapt their distribution strategy.	Not Significant
H4d	The greater the difference of government regulations between home and export market, the greater the likelihood that Malaysian exporters will adapt their pricing strategy.	Significant
H5a	The greater the cultural differences between Malaysia and export market, the greater the degree of product strategy adaptation of Malaysian exporters.	Not Significant
H5b	The greater the cultural differences between Malaysia and export market, the greater the degree of promotion strategy adaptation of Malaysian exporters.	Significant
H5c	The greater the cultural differences between Malaysia and export market, the greater the degree of distribution strategy adaptation of Malaysian exporters.	Not Significant
H5d	The greater the cultural differences between Malaysia and export market, the greater the degree of pricing strategy adaptation of Malaysian exporters.	Not Significant
H6a	The greater the economic difference between the exporters' home market and foreign market, the greater the level of adaptation of product strategy of Malaysian exporters.	Significant\

No	Hypothesis	Result
H6b	The greater the economic difference between the exporters' home market and foreign market, the greater the level of adaptation of promotion strategy of Malaysian exporters.	Not Significant
H6c	The greater the economic difference between the exporters' home market and foreign market, the greater the level of adaptation of distribution strategy of Malaysian exporters.	Not Significant
H6d	The greater the economic difference between the exporters' home market and foreign market, the greater the level of adaptation of pricing strategy of Malaysian exporters.	Not Significant
H7a	The greater the negative image of the exporting country (Malaysia), the greater the likelihood that Malaysian exporters will adapt their product strategy to foreign markets.	Not Significant
H7b	The greater the negative image of the exporting country (Malaysia), the greater the likelihood that Malaysian exporters will adapt their promotion strategy to foreign markets.	Not Significant
H7c	The greater the negative image of the exporting country (Malaysia), the greater the likelihood that Malaysian exporters will adapt their distribution strategy to foreign markets.	Not Significant
H7d	The greater the negative image of the exporting country (Malaysia), the greater the likelihood that Malaysian exporters will adapt their pricing strategy to foreign markets.	Not Significant
H8a	The greater the difference in physical conditions between the local and foreign market, the greater the likelihood that Malaysian exporters will adapt their product strategy in foreign markets.	Significant
H8b	The difference in physical conditions between the local and foreign market, the greater the likelihood that Malaysian exporters will adapt their promotion strategy in foreign markets.	Significant
H8c	The difference in physical conditions between the local and foreign market, the greater the likelihood that Malaysian exporters will adapt their distribution strategy in foreign markets.	Significant
H8d	The difference in physical conditions between the local and foreign market, the greater the likelihood that Malaysian exporters will adapt their pricing strategy in foreign markets.	Not Significant
H9a	The greater the difference between the marketing infrastructure of the exporters' local and foreign market, the greater the level of adaptation of the product strategy of Malaysian exporters.	Not Significant
H9b	The greater the difference between the marketing infrastructure of the exporters' local and foreign market, the greater the level of adaptation of the promotion strategy of Malaysian exporters.	Significant
H9c	The greater the difference between the marketing infrastructure of the exporters' local and foreign market, the greater the level of adaptation of the distribution strategy of Malaysian exporters.	Significant
H9d	The greater the difference between the marketing infrastructure of the exporters' local and foreign market, the greater the level of adaptation of the pricing strategy of Malaysian exporters.	Significant
H10-1	The marketing mix adaptation mediates the effect of international experience on the performance of Malaysian export companies.	Significant
H10-2	The marketing mix adaptation mediates the effect of technology intensity on the performance of Malaysian export companies.	Not Significant
H10-3	The marketing mix adaptation mediates the effect of competition level of the industry on performance of Malaysian export companies.	Not Significant
H10-4	The marketing mix adaptation mediates the effect of differences of government regulations between home and export market on performance of Malaysian export companies.	Not Significant

No	Hypothesis	Result
H10-5	The marketing mix adaptation mediates the effect of cultural differences between Malaysia and export market on performance of Malaysian export companies.	Not Significant
H10-6	The marketing mix adaptation mediates the effect of economic differences between the exporters' home market and foreign market on performance of Malaysian export companies.	Significant
H10-7	The marketing mix adaptation mediates the effect of the negative image of the exporting country (Malaysia) on performance of Malaysian export companies.	Not Significant
H10-8	The marketing mix adaptation mediates the effect of differences in physical conditions between the exporters' home market and foreign market on performance of Malaysian export companies.	Significant
H10-9	The marketing mix adaptation mediates the effect of differences in marketing infrastructure between the exporters' home market and foreign market on performance of Malaysian export companies.	Significant
H11-a	The greater the level of product strategy adaptation, the better the Malaysian exporters' performance.	Significant
H11-b	The greater the level of promotion strategy adaptation, the better the Malaysian exporters' performance.	Significant
H11-c	The greater the level of distribution strategy adaptation, the better the Malaysian exporters' performance.	Significant
H11-d	The greater the level of pricing strategy adaptation, the better the Malaysian exporters' performance.	Not Significant

In sum, this chapter concluded with a detailed section on hypotheses testing in which the hypotheses of this study were subject to testing to reveal whether they were significant or rejected.

Five

Discussion and Conclusions

OVERVIEW OF FINDINGS AND DISCUSSION

Chapter 4 presented the findings of the present research. In this section, a summary of these findings are presented. To make it easier and direct, the findings of the study are outlined in a set of tables. Three main tables are presented regarding the three main questions in the study. The first Table 5.1 outlines the effect of the antecedent factors on the degree of adaptation of the marketing mix in the Malaysian export companies. Table 5.2 outlines the impact of antecedent factors on the performance of Malaysian export companies, through the mediating influence of marketing mix adaptation. Finally, Table 5.3 outlines the findings of the impact of marketing mix adaptation on the export performance of Malaysian export companies.

Table 5.1 outlines the direct link between the antecedent factors and the marking mix adaptation. In other words, this Table outlines the impact of international experience, technology intensity, competition level, government regulation, cultural differences, economic differences, country image, physical conditions, and marketing infrastructure on the marketing mix adaption that is represented by product adaptation, promotion adaptation, distribution adaptation and pricing adaptation.

It can be seen from the Table 5.1 above that some antecedent factors were found to have significant effect on marketing mix adaptation strategies. On the other hand, some other antecedent factors were not found to have a significant impact on the marketing mix adaptation strategies. The following section provides a detailed discussion about these findings.

Effect of International Experience on the Degree of Adaptation of the Marketing Mix in the Malaysian Export Companies

The current research aimed to identify the effects that international experience has on the level of adaptation of the four main elements of the marketing mix.

Table 5.1: The effect of the antecedent factors on the degree of adaptation of the marketing mix in the Malaysian export companies

Path	*Effect*	*Path Coefficient*	*T. Statistics*	*Result*
EXP -> PRD	Direct	0.030	1.393	Not Significant
EXP -> PRM	Direct	0.026	0.920	Not Significant
EXP -> DIS	Direct	0.088	2.769**	Significant
EXP -> PRI	Direct	0.008	0.382	Not Significant
TEC -> PRD	Direct	0.005	0.083	Not Significant
TEC -> PRM	Direct	0.001	0.023	Not Significant
TEC -> DIS	Direct	–0.049	0.638	Not Significant
TEC -> PRI	Direct	0.007	0.103	Not Significant
COM -> PRD	Direct	0.070	0.828	Not Significant
COM -> PRM	Direct	0.018	0.328	Not Significant
COM -> DIS	Direct	–0.033	0.448	Not Significant
COM -> PRI	Direct	0.061	0.916	Not Significant
GOV -> PRD	Direct	0.169	2.263*	Significant
GOV -> PRM	Direct	0.041	0.645	Not Significant
GOV -> DIS	Direct	–0.051	0.716	Not Significant
GOV -> PRI	Direct	0.284	3.499***	Significant
CUL -> PRD	Direct	0.022	0.339	Not Significant
CUL -> PRM	Direct	0.191	2.246*	Significant
CUL -> DIS	Direct	–0.013	0.193	Not Significant
CUL -> PRI	Direct	0.112	1.120	Not Significant
ECO -> PRD	Direct	0.254	2.791**	Significant
ECO -> PRM	Direct	0.071	0.569	Not Significant
ECO -> DIS	Direct	0.151	1.631	Not Significant
ECO -> PRI	Direct	0.045	0.619	Not Significant
IMG -> PRD	Direct	–0.010	0.137	Not Significant
IMG -> PRM	Direct	–0.017	0.210	Not Significant
IMG -> DIS	Direct	0.023	0.393	Not Significant
IMG -> PRI	Direct	0.011	0.137	Not Significant
PHY -> PRD	Direct	0.358	3.879***	Significant
PHY -> PRM	Direct	0.284	3.457***	Significant
PHY -> DIS	Direct	0.465	4.672***	Significant
PHY -> PRI	Direct	–0.031	0.488	Not Significant
INF -> PRD	Direct	0.007	0.106	Not Significant
INF -> PRM	Direct	0.254	3.943***	Significant
INF -> DIS	Direct	0.287	3.798***	Significant
INF -> PRI	Direct	0.355	3.983***	Significant

International experience plays an imperative role in the ability of a company to penetrate into new markets as well as sustain these markets. This study sought to determine if international experience affects the adaptation of the marketing mix in Malaysia. The relationship between international experience and the four elements of the marketing mix were evaluated.

Hypothesis H1a states that the greater the international experience, the greater the likelihood that Malaysian exporters will adapt their product strategy. The result of this hypothesis was found to be not significant. This can be attributed to the fact that most of the companies selling products abroad do not alter them so as to suit the local market. Previous research indicates that most of the companies alter their products so as to suit the local market. This in turn promotes consumer satisfaction level and results in the sale of more products. From the research carried out, it was found that most of the respondents did not use their knowledge and experience in international trade to alter their products so as to suit the local market abroad. The results contradicted what previous researchers found, i.e., most of the international companies rely on the information from the local market to develop products that will be generally acceptable by the consumers (Douglas & Craig, 1989). Prior research indicates that companies rebrand their products, repack them and also perform other product alterations, so as to suit the target market (Cavusgil, Zou & Naidu, 1993; Hill & Still, 1984). It is therefore imperative that the current companies be sensitized on the need to change the products based on their understanding of the market. There are many predicaments that may hinder product adaptations as a result of international experience. Various researchers indicate that most of the firms are faced with tough decisions whether to adapt to the local market or to standardize their products. Various researchers indicate that some companies favor standardization of products as opposed to adaptation. Both adaptation and standardization have merits and demerits and the choice of the two may not be determined by the company's international knowledge and market. It has also been found that the adaptation and standardization are affected by other factors, such as the internal and external environment that the company operates in, the competition and international experience of the company. Thus, experience plays a trivial role in the determination of whether to standardize or adapt. Various researchers advance the idea of standardization as being more superior compared to adaptation. The merits of standardization encompass: economies-of-scale, uniformity in productions, cost savings, products and services are consistent and of high quality, reduction in the management complexities, technological improvements, improved communications between the company and distributors, homogenization, ability to improve their brand and the firms are able to gain immense knowledge, among other factors (Carpano and Chrisman, 1995; Walters, 1986; Theodosiu and Katsikeas, 2001; Schuh, 2000). From these aforementioned advantages, it can be seen that most of the firms may feel that it is not obligatory to adapt their products to the local market despite their long experience in international trade.

There are several factors that affect a firm's choice to adapt. Despite a company's experience and realizations of the need to adapt, other factors may hinder the adaptation process. Some of these factors include performance measures, size of the company, experience in the market and the volume of international sales that the company makes. All these factors play a pivotal role in deciding whether a company should adapt its products for the local market. From this research, it is evident that the product adaptation is not one of the determinants of the need to adapt for Malaysian companies. Another reason why the firms in this study may have chosen not to adapt is the market characteristics. From the data obtained, it was found out that most of the firms export to many markets and this could serve as a hindrance to adapting as changing products in all the markets may be tedious and expensive for the companies.

For example, Hypothesis H1b stated that the greater the international experience, the greater the likelihood that Malaysian exporters will adapt their promotion strategy. The result of this hypothesis was reported to be not significant. Various studies have shown that multinational companies use different tactics to promote and advertise different products. These messages are tailor-made so as to capture the local market. This is imperative as customers are able to identify the product with their local needs and settings. The respondents however indicated that there is no significance between international companies and the promotion messages used by these companies. Again, it can be seen that most of the firms in Malaysia do not adjust/adapt their advertising and promotion messages based on their international experience; rather, these messages are influenced by other factors. In total, about 77 per cent of the companies had an experience of more than 20 years in the market. Yet, most of the companies did not find this experience as being useful in formulating the product promotional strategies. This can be attributed to the fact only 9.5 per cent of the companies have a distribution center in the export country. The remaining products reach the export market through direct sales, use of an agent, use of export management companies, and use of home companies. All these sellers are in direct contact with the customers at the foreign market and hence the companies in Malaysia do not deal with the consumers in the export countries directly. This means that they are not in a good position to formulate advertising jargons and promotional strategies suitable to the target market.

Hypothesis H1c stated that the greater the international experience, the greater the likelihood that Malaysian exporters will adapt their distribution strategy. The results of this study indicated that there is a significant effect of experience on the distribution channels used by companies. One of the main factors affecting international trade is the distribution channels used by the company. These affect the ability of the products to reach the consumer, availability of the products, promotions and the final price of the item. It is therefore imperative that companies choose the most appropriate distribution channel to ensure products reach the consumer on time and at the right place.

Distribution channels are complex and need careful selection and management. This experience in the international market therefore plays an imperative role as those experienced know the merits and demerits of each of the distribution methods and are able to use the most appropriate distribution channel for the products. International experience also helps companies select the best distributors who will ensure that their products are transferred from producer to the consumer. Thus, most of the respondents agreed that experience was crucial in determining the best distribution channels. International experience is seen as giving companies an upper hand in the determination of the most appropriate route that the products and services pass through. Previous researchers agree that international experience plays a significant role in the determination of the adaptation of the distributions channel.

Hypothesis H1d stated that the greater the international experience, the greater the likelihood that Malaysian exporters will adapt their pricing strategy. The result of this hypothesis was found to be not significant. Pricing of commodities in the international market is influenced by a number of factors. Various authors indicate that there are a number of factors that must be considered when setting prices for the international market. These factors can be classified into four different groups: (1) the firm level factors encompassing factors such as marketing mix elements, the cost structure and the firm's strategic objectives. The marketing mix elements include factors such as the consumer of the product and the process involved in manufacture of these products. These two must be taken into consideration as the business must make profit. A product must be linked to a particular value and this depends upon several factors, the most influential being the amount used to produce the product and distribute it to the final consumers; (2) the product specific factors such as substitutes, products from competitors, product quality, service delivery, cost of shipping the products and financing operations. These factors must be taken into consideration when determining the final price of the product; (3) the consumer's ability to purchase the product, the price of the product in the market, distribution channels used and the marketing costs; and (4) the macro environmental factors such as inflation, government policy, and competition.

It can be seen that so many factors must be taken into consideration before the final price of a product is determined. Most of these factors do not require the company to have great deal of experience in the international market. For example, if a company wants to export products to Australia, the pricing will be determined by considering the government regulations in that country, the price of competitors 'products, quality and many more factors. All these factors do not require international experience for the firm to be successful. Another reason why most of the respondents indicated that pricing is not an important factor is the fact that most of them rely on distributors who buy products from them and they sell them to the consumers. Only 28 per cent of the total products are sold directly to the final consumers and the rest of the products (72%) are sold through distributors who may price the products based on the local market conditions. Perhaps some of the main areas in pricing that may require significant expertise in the international trade are price discrimination and market segmentations. These two require that the firm understands the market fully before setting the price of the product. Again, this information can be obtained by conducting a thorough market survey before rolling out the product into the market. This shows that the contribution of experience in international market in setting the product price is trivial and of not much importance.

Another factor that may have contributed to the international experience not affecting pricing is the fact that some companies have a uniform price for their products. This has led to standardization of commodity price. This is seen in most of the companies all over the world where the store prices for the commodities are of the same quality and price throughout. For example, clothing stores and motor dealers have a uniform price which is set by the companies and all customers buy at this price (Terpstra, 2000). This would mean the experience of the firm would not affect the pricing in any way as there are no price discriminations in the market. Thus, standardization of prices can be said to result in the firm's inability to adapt to the local market through their international expertise.

From the research finding, it was found that international experience affects the export performance of the firm. The main effects are in the identification and utilization of distribution channels. Most respondents felt that firms that have been in the international trade for long, have experience in identifying the right agents, dealers, clearing and forwarding companies and this enables their product to reach the target market at the right time, at the right place and in a good condition. By the very fact that they have dealt with many agents in the new countries, makes them have a market advantage over the new entrants. Logistical expertise which is gained through experience and using qualified people, thus plays an imperative role in determining the success of international companies based in Malaysia.

The Effect of Technology Intensity on the Degree of Adaptation of the Marketing Mix in the Malaysian Export Companies

The second factor that was investigated was the use of technology as a tool for fostering increased international trade in Malaysia. The technology intensity can be defined as the investments/money that are spent by the companies in improving their products or the process of innovating new products and processes. The portion of money that is channeled to innovations and new development is referred to as the technological intensity. There are various classifications of companies depending on their technological intensity. These groups include high, medium high, medium low and low technology companies. Various researches indicate that technology intensity is an imperative factor affecting the company's performance at all levels. This study, sought to establish whether technology intensity is considered an important factor affecting the export market in Malaysia.

Hypothesis H2a stated that the technology intensity of the industry is positively associated with the degree of product adaptation of Malaysian exporters. The result of this hypothesis was found to be not significant. This is not consistent with the findings by Cavusgil & Zou (1994) who indicate that product and promotions adaptation are affected by the competitiveness of a product and the brand development, and these rely on innovations and product differentiation. For companies to attract and retain customers, they must build a reputable brand image and develop high quality products that will satisfy the customer's utility. This necessitates continuous improvement of the products and this is done through innovation. This can be attributed to the fact that most companies rely on different strategies in order to gain competitive advantages. One of these methods is the development of new innovative products and service delivery at the local market. However, for Malaysian exporters, it was observed that new technological methods are not used to improve products so as to suit a particular market. This can be attributed to the fact that the companies have standard products suitable for the global market. Companies may choose standardization as opposed to adaptation. In Malaysia, companies have opted to have high quality standard products sold to all the markets. This is consistent with previous findings where it was noted that the exporters do not use their international expertise to adapt their products.

Another factor that could have influenced their inability to innovate is lack of feedback from the customers. It can be seen that only 28 per cent of the total export products are directly distributed to the customers. This means that most of the importing customers deal with agents, retailers and other distributors who may not convey feedback from the client and trigger the Malaysian exporters to alter their products in response to a particular market. The issue of product adaptation is also expensive and tedious. Research done with European companies indicate that most of these companies only choose simple adaptation, such as repacking and rebranding, but not the change of product specifications and quality. Thus, cost is a major hindrance to both technological developments and adaptation.

Hypothesis H2b stated that the technology intensity is negatively associated with the degree of promotion adaptation of Malaysian exporters. The result of this hypothesis was found to be not significant. The level of technological sophistications could be used by a company as leverage to create advanced promotional strategies targeting the local market. However, for Malaysian exporters, there is no relationship between technological advancement and promotion strategy adaptation. This can be attributed to the fact that most of the exporters are not well linked with the target customers and hence, do not participate in the development of sales and promotions of products abroad. It would be prudent therefore for future researchers to evaluate if these firms actually promote their products overseas. One of the major strategies adopted by most of the multinational companies which export products to various countries, is the development and adaptation of new and different promotional strategies that target the local market. However, the results obtained in this study are in contradiction of these facts. Various authors also indicate that it is necessary for firms to formulate promotion strategies that target a particular region so as to effectively communicate and capture the customers 'attention. The size of the firm also affects the technological intensity and the degree of promotion strategies used abroad. The process of creating promotional strategies targeting the local consumers is expensive and requires a lot of resources. Only large multinational companies with regional headquarters and their own distribution outlets are able to advertise locally. However, using advanced technology such as social media, like the internet, exporters in Malaysia can be able to formulate promotional strategies targeting the local markets.

Hypothesis H2c stated that the technology intensity is negatively associated with the degree of distribution adaptation of Malaysian exporters. Again, the result of this hypothesis was found to be not significant. The technology intensity does not have a direct impact on the choice of distributors and having sophisticated methods of managing distributions networks could enable the firm to effectively manage their distribution network. The lack of relationship can be attributed to the fact that the company does not control the distribution network of the foreign companies. In fact, only 29 per cent of the total products are sold through direct sales while 6.5 per cent are sold through joint ventures and 9.5 through subsidiary in the target country. This means that most of the innovations that Malaysian companies may develop to promote and enhance their distribution networks and adapt to the local market are hampered by the choices and decisions of the other companies of the distribution network.

Hypothesis: The technology intensity is positively associated with the degree of pricing adaptation of Malaysian exporters. Again, there was no significant relationship between the two factors indicating that the level of technology does not affect the changes in price at the target market. The results are in contrast with what other researchers have found that competitiveness and brand familiarity affect the price competitiveness of products. The use of better technology and use of innovations in the distribution and supply networks are likely to drive the prices of commodities lower and this would result in the reduction in prices. For example, a company may opt to produce at the target export country so as to minimize the shipping, handling costs and other costs and this would reduce the product cost. The Malaysian exporter may not be in control of the final market and hence, it is difficult for them to use technological solutions to reduce or adjust prices at the target market. Another reason could be standardization of prices at their outlets.

Standardization ensures uniformity in price and this may hinder selective pricing strategies.

In conclusion, it can be seen that the technology intensity does not affect the international performance of Malaysian export companies as it does not influence or mediate in any of the four marketing mix elements. Therefore, Malaysian exporters at any level of technology can participate in the export business successfully. However, further research should be carried out to compare Malaysian firms with other companies in the world who use technology intensity as leverage to better adapt to the four marketing mix elements. Lack of high levels of technology may be deemed by the respondents as being unimportant because the idea has not been exploited by any of the exporters.

The Effect of Competition Level on the Degree of Adaptation of the Marketing Mix in the Malaysian Export Companies

In the modern market, competition by other firms is a major consideration in determining the kind of adaptation that companies make. Ideally, competition should actually drive the process of product differentiations, market segmentations and price adjustments. In this study, the relationship between the competition level and the adaptation of the marketing mix elements was checked.

Hypothesis H3a indicated that the competition level of the industry is related to the degree of product adaptation of Malaysian exporters. The results showed that there is no significant relationship between the two factors. The results are in contradiction to most of the research findings which indicate that increased competition results in companies adapting different strategies so as to compete in the market. The results indicated that even though there may be high competition in the export countries, Malaysian exporters do not actually differentiate their products so as to gain competitive advantages. One of the reasons could be lack of interaction with the local consumers and inadequate market surveys at the target countries. Another factor that may hamper any efforts for product differentiations and adaptation is standardization. Most of the products that are exported are too hard to differentiate and existing legislation at the target importing nations may have set standards. For example, items such as computer parts, electronics, fruits, foods, fertilizers, minerals and other products have regulations and minimum requirements that must be met before exporting or importing these commodities. It then becomes difficult for the exporters to differentiate these products.

Hypothesis H3b stated that the competition level of the industry is related to the degree of promotion adaptation of Malaysian exporters. Again, the results indicated that there is no significant relationship between the competition level and the adaptation of the promotional strategies used by the company. This is in contrast to researchers who show that high competition levels result in aggressive marketing campaigns so as to reach the target market. Cavusgil *et al's.* (1993) findings indicate that export market competitiveness, has a significant effect on product and/or promotion adaptation and Chung's (2003) findings indicate that competitive environment has a significant effect on the marketing mix standardization. The results may have been caused by lack of direct involvement of the exporting companies in the local market. The exporters seem to have no direct link with the customers and hence no promotions are carried out by the companies in the foreign countries.

Hypothesis H3c stated that the competition level of the industry is related to the degree of distribution adaptation of Malaysian exporters. Again, it was found that competition did not significantly affect the exporter's choice of the distribution network. This is in contrast to what most of the researchers found, i.e., the level and number of competitors in the international market affect the choice of distribution network. This result is different from Chung's (2002) findings that competitive environment has a significant effect on distribution adaptation. Multinational companies choose appropriate distribution networks and adapt to local environment so as to maximize on profits. This is however not the case with Malaysian exporters. These findings could be attributed to the type of export products and the exporters having no direct contact with consumers.

Hypothesis H3d stated that the competition level of the industry is related to the degree of price adaptation of Malaysian exporters. The results indicated that there are no significant relations between the competition level and the pricing adaptation. The results are different from Cavusgil & Zou's (1994) and Chung's (2002) findings that competitive environment has a significant effect on distribution, promotion, and price adaptation. Most of the international companies set their prices based on the local market in that country. However, in this case, most of the exporters can be said to have standardized the products they sell such that price differentiation is not possible. In addition, the manufacturers may not be the final product resellers and this makes them unable to control the price of the final product to the customers. For example, exported food items may be sold to distributors who may sell them to malls, who in turn distribute them to the final consumers. This leaves the exporter in no position to change prices based on the competition level. Thus, it can be seen that the exporters' pricing strategy is not based on the competition in the local market.

In conclusion, it can be seen that the level of competition did not affect or mediate in the adaptations of the different marketing mix elements. There are many factors that could have caused this occurrence. First, there may be limited competition levels for the products being exported; secondly companies in Malaysia may opt to standardize their products and promotional strategies so that the effects in the foreign country are not considered important during the formulations of the marketing mix. It may also be very expensive for the parent company to carry out advertisements, product differentiations and pricing for all the countries that they supply to. This could have resulted in the companies opting to standardize their products as opposed to adapting to the local market.

The Effect of Government Regulations on the Degree of Adaptation of the Marketing Mix in the Malaysian Export Companies

The government legal and regulatory framework affects and controls international trade. In the study, the researchers sought to determine whether government regulations affect export performance by mediating the marketing mix factors.

Hypothesis H4a specified that the greater the difference of government regulations between home and export market, the greater the likelihood that Malaysian exporters will adapt their product strategy. This means the difference in government regulations between home and export market would result in Malaysian export companies adapting their product strategy. The result of this hypothesis was reported to be significant. The results are consistent with the previous research as changes in the government regulations are likely to affect the products that are produced. Government regulations are likely to set the quality and quantity of the products to be imported in the country and the exporters have no choice than to adapt their products to suit the government's requirements. The level of adaptation is affected by the difference in regulations between the exporting and the importing countries. If the regulations by the importing country are less stringent as compared to those of Malaysia, then less product differentiation is required as the product already meets the safety and other legal requirements. However, if the importing country has more stringent rules on quality as compared to Malaysia (for example Britain importing products from Malaysia), it is expected that the exporters must change and adapt their products so that they may be allowed to sell them in the foreign market. The results obtained are consistent with Johnson & Arunthanes' (1995) findings that Government regulations significantly affect product adaptation; Cavusgil *et al.* (1993) and Chung (2002) also found out that government regulations has a significant effect on distribution and product adaptation.

Hypothesis H4b specified that the greater the differences of government regulations between home and export market, the greater the likelihood that Malaysian exporters will adapt their promotional strategy. This hypothesis could not be verified and the results indicate that the promotional strategies are not affected by the differences in government regulations between the two countries. This result is different from Johnson & Arunthanes' (1995) findings that government regulations significantly affect product adaptation, as well as Cavusgil *et al.*'s (1993) and Chung's (2002) findings that government regulations had a significant effect on distribution and product adaptation. Basically, a government regulation only stipulates the quality and general conditions that exporters must meet for them to sell products to that country. Some countries also issue quotas which specify the amount of goods they can receive from a certain region. However, it is the duty of the exporter to determine what promotional strategies to use so as to ensure that his or her products reach the final consumers. Some exporters rely on their agents, and thus are not involved in formulating promotional strategies in the foreign country. This explains why most Malaysian exporters believe that government regulations have no effects on the choice of the promotion messages adopted by them.

Hypothesis H4c stated that the greater the difference of government regulations between home and export market, the greater the likelihood that Malaysian exporters will adapt their distribution strategy. The results indicated that there is no relationship between the differences of government regulations between home and export market and its distribution strategy adaptation. As a result, H4c was not significant. As mentioned earlier, government regulations do not affect the choice of distribution network to be used by the company. The government only serves as a regulator of the amount and quality of the export products. Due to this factor, most of the exporters are free to choose the distribution network to use so long as the government controls and regulations are not breached. However, government regulations on labor laws, minimum wages, tax laws and other rules may increase the final products cost, triggering exporters to identify new distribution channels which are more cost effective. In this case however, the government regulations do not affect the distribution channels as most of the exporters rely on the already established distribution channels to market their products. The results are not consistent with what Cavusgil *et al.* (1993) and Chung (2002) found that government regulations have a significant effect on distribution and product adaptation.

Hypothesis H4d stated that the greater the difference of government regulations between home and export market, the greater the likelihood that Malaysian exporters will adapt their pricing strategy. The results indicated that there was a relationship between the government regulations and the pricing strategies used by exporters. The results are consistent with Johnson & Arunthanes' (1995) findings that government regulations significantly affect product adaptation, Cavusgil *et al.'s* (1993) and Chung's (2002) findings that government regulations had a significant effect on pricing adaptation.

Government regulations on the export products and services are mainly aimed at improving the quality of these products. If there is a difference in regulations between the two countries, the exporters must add more features to improve the quality of products and these results indirect increase in expenses, which in turn result in increased product costs and a change in the pricing strategy.

Effect of Cultural Differences on the Degree of Adaptation of the Marketing Mix in the Malaysian Export Companies

Cultural differences between the different nations play an imperative role in determining the export performance of a company. Cultural differences between the importing and exporting countries should ideally affect the level of marketing mix adaptation. Companies must formulate their products so as to match the cultural needs of the importing country. In this study the effects of culture on export performance was examined.

Hypothesis H5a specified that the greater the cultural differences between Malaysia and the export market, the greater the degree of product strategy adaptation of Malaysian exporters. This hypothesis was not verified showing that the cultural differences between Malaysia and export market do not affect Malaysian export companies to adapt their product strategy. As a result, H5a was not significant. Various researchers document the need for foreign companies to consider the cultural background of the foreign market when adapting product strategies (Bradley, 2002). Bradley (2002) formulated a matrix showing how cultures of different nations should be used during product and decision making

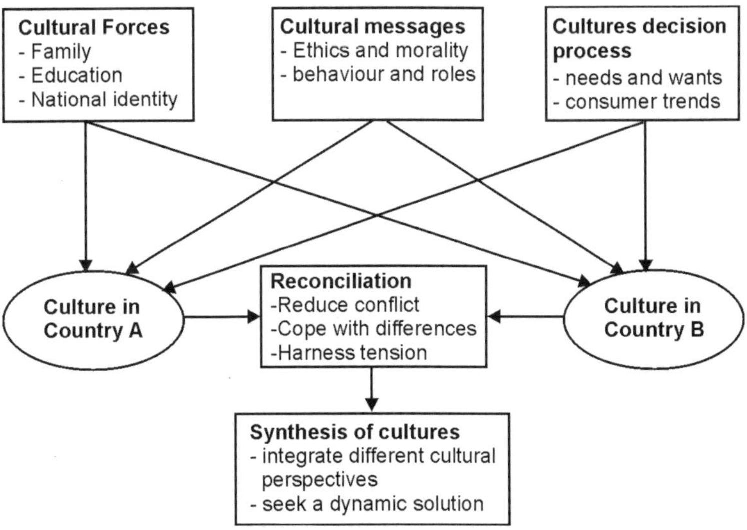

Figure 5.1: The Cultural Influence on the Exporter's Process

When formulating the product strategy, it is necessary to consider the cultural background of the foreign nation. In this case however, the respondents indicated that the cultural differences do not play a significant role in adaptation of product strategy. This can be caused by the nature of products; for example, if one considers products such as computers, electronics, fruits and other food stuffs, cultural differences cannot result in changes to these products. A TV will be marketed as a TV in all places of the world regardless of the culture. Fruits will always remain fruits in all the different cultures. Thus, in this case, most of the products are the same in different cultures.

Hypothesis H5b specified that the greater the cultural differences between Malaysia and the export market, the greater the degree of promotion strategy adaptation of Malaysian exporters. This hypothesis was verified showing that cultural differences between home and export market will lead Malaysian export companies to adapt their promotion strategy. When formulating the promotional strategies, it is imperative that these strategies are developed with the target audience in mind. This calls for development of promotional messages and strategies which are in line with the cultural norms of the society. According to Bradley (2002), promotional strategies must be formulated taking into considerations the ethics, norms, morality and culture of the exporting and importing countries. The results obtained are in line with previous researchers who indicate that cultural environment affects the marketing mix adaptation as more specific strategies must be formulated in line with the cultural norms of a given place. A cultural influence of a county encompasses cultural forces, messages and the customer decision process. Cultural forces manifest themselves in form of family, education and national identity. When formulating strategies, the foreign companies must analyze the cultural differences between the two countries and develop strategies that reconcile the two cultures. Research done by Cavusgil & Zou (1994) indicates that cultural specificity affects the product, promotions adaptation, price competitiveness and the support that foreign distributors adopt. Cavusgil *et al.* (1993) found that cultural specificity of products has a significant effect on product and/or promotion adaptation.

For example, hypothesis H5c specified that the greater the cultural differences between Malaysia and export market, the greater the degree of distribution strategy adaptation of Malaysian exporters. This hypothesis was not verified and the cultural differences between Malaysia and export market does not affect Malaysian export companies to adapt their distribution strategy. The results clearly indicated that culture does not determine the choice of the distributions channel that a company chooses to adapt. The distribution channels are mainly affected by the price of commodity and the efficiency of the distribution in availing the products to the customer at the right time and place. The results are in contradiction to what various researchers have found that cultural specificity affects the marketing mix adaptation and specifically it influences the distribution network (Cavusgil & Zou, 1994).

Hypothesis H5d specified that the greater the cultural differences between Malaysia and export market, the greater the degree of pricing strategy adaptation of Malaysian exporters. This hypothesis was not verified, and thus, cultural differences between Malaysia and export market do not affect Malaysian export companies to adapt their pricing strategy. The results obtained indicated that cultural differences between the two countries do not affect the pricing strategies adopted by the firm. The results are not consistent with the previous researchers who show that culture affects the marketing mix and also the price competitiveness of a product. The culture of the people may influence the consumer behavior. Markets located in developing areas have most of the people adapting the culture of purchasing lowly priced products while those in rich and developed nations purchase highly priced products. This indicates that price differentiation might be a necessary choice.

Effect of Economic Differences on the Degree of Adaptation of the Marketing Mix in the Malaysian Export Companies

Economic differences between the export and import countries play an imperative role in international trade. The economic distance between two trading nations affects the ability of citizens to purchase products. If two countries have a wide economic gap between them, such as a developed nation exporting products to a low income country (under-developed), the price of the products may be too high for the local residents to afford and this may result in some adaptation. The effects of economic differences on marketing mix adaptations were evaluated and the results obtained were as follows:

Hypothesis H6a specified that the greater the economic differences between the exporter's home market and foreign market, the greater the level of adaptation of product strategy of Malaysian exporters. This hypothesis was verified and thus the differences in economic conditions between exporter's home market and foreign market would lead the export companies to adapt their products to suit these differences. When Malaysian exporters are trading with low income countries, they need to alter their products so as to have lower quality and less expansive products. When trading with a richer nation, they need to enhance product quality and other features. Economic differences also represent the level of sophistication that countries have and this should also be reflected in the products sold to them. Exporters must ensure the quality of products sold to the high-end market.

Hypothesis H6b specified that the greater the economic differences between the exporters' home market and foreign market, the greater the level of adaptation of promotion strategy of Malaysian exporters. This hypothesis was not verified and the economic differences between Malaysia and export market do not affect Malaysian export companies to adapt their promotion strategy. The economic differences between the two nations have an impact but do not affect the promotional strategies used. Adaptation to promotional strategies must be tailor-made based on the economic status of a country. The results obtained in this study, however, showed that Malaysian exporters' promotional strategies are not affected by the economic differences of the two countries. This could be attributed to the fact that most of the companies sell their products through agents and other companies in the foreign market, and thus they do not specialize in marketing in these areas. The results are different from Chung's (2002) findings that economic development has significant effect on promotional strategies.

Hypothesis H6c specified that the greater the economic differences between the exporters' home market and foreign market, the greater the level of adaptation of distribution strategy of Malaysian exporters. The results showed that there is no relationship between the economic differences and the adaptation of the distribution strategy. These results contradict what previous research has shown that economic differences between two nations is expected to increase the cost of distributing products and this may force the companies to change distribution channels. However, in this case, economic differences of the countries that Malaysia exports to may have a small economic difference and this means that the exporters can still maintain the same distribution channels. Researchers indicate that firms may identify target markets that need little or no modifications of products and the distribution network and this selective market identification means that most exporters will prefer to choose an export market with little or no adjustments to the marketing mix (Czinkota and Ronkainen, 2004).

Hypothesis H6d specified that the greater the economic difference between the exporters' home market and foreign market, the greater the level of adaptation of pricing strategy of Malaysian exporters. This hypothesis was not verified showing there is no relationship between the two. These results are different from Chung's (2002) findings that economic development has significant effect on pricing adaptation. The differences in economic conditions between different nations can result in changes in the pricing strategies. However, in cases where the competition is uniform, the pricing strategies may not change due to economic differences in the two nations. In this case, the pricing strategies do not affect the adaptation in pricing strategy. This is due to having a standardized pricing strategy and the fact that the economic differences between the importing countries and Malaysia are small. This means that the economic distance between the two nations is small and exporters are likely to use the same pricing strategy as those in Malaysia. The research also indicated that the economic differences in the two nations cannot result in changes in pricing strategy; this may be due to the fact that the exporters are not in direct link with the consumers and rely on agents and distributors for advertising to the local consumers. Another reason that could have caused lack of pricing strategy is homogenization of products, i.e., all the products being exported are of the same quality and specifications. For example, if an electronic component costing $1000 is made for export, the price must be higher than this price irrespective of the market where the product is sold.

Effect of Country Image on the Degree of Adaptation of the Marketing Mix in the Malaysian Export Companies

Country image affects the acceptability of goods in a particular country. Goods from one country may be preferred as opposed to another country. The exporters must take this into consideration when developing their marketing mix. The preference of products from a given country thus affects the export performance. In this study, an investigation on the impacts of country image on the adaptation of marketing mix by Malaysian exporters was undertaken.

Hypothesis H7a specified that the greater the negative image of the exporting country (Malaysia), the greater the likelihood that Malaysian exporters will adapt their product strategy to foreign markets. The hypothesis was not verified. This could have been because most of the countries where exporters operate, consider Malaysia as a superior nation, where they can get products. Most of the exporters who responded, indicated that they have been exporting for more than 20 years, and this could have resulted in the positive perception that most of the importers have. Exporters also choose target markets based on the ease of operations and this results in standardization as opposed to adaptation. The findings are not in line with previous research which shows that country image affects the product market adaptation (Park, 2006).

Hypothesis H7b indicated the greater the negative image of the exporting country (Malaysia), the greater the likelihood that Malaysian exporters will adapt their promotion strategy to foreign markets. The results indicate that negative image does not affect the export company's promotional strategy. The findings could be due to the fact that the export companies are not wholly involved in promotions in the foreign countries, and hence the impact of country image does not feature too much. These findings contradict those of Park (2006) which indicates that there is significant relationship between country image and promotional strategy adaptation.

Hypothesis H7c specified that the greater the negative image of the exporting country (Malaysia), the greater the likelihood that Malaysian exporters will adapt their distribution strategy to foreign markets. This hypothesis was rejected showing that there is no relation between the country image and the likelihood to adapt new distribution strategies. The main reasons for this could be that most of the exporters use their experience to select the distribution lines and this is not affected by the reputations of the original country especially when the distribution channels at the target market are determined by the companies located abroad.

Hypothesis H7d specified that the greater the negative image of the exporting country (Malaysia), the greater the likelihood that Malaysian exporters will adapt their pricing strategy to foreign markets. The hypothesis was rejected as it could not be verified meaning that the pricing strategy is not affected by country image. The pricing strategy, in this case, is affected by other factors such as government policy as the exporters and the customers have no direct link. Price standardization could also result in fixed prices as well as the issue of having uniform competition in the foreign market. The results obtained are different from what Park (2006) found that the exporting country's image affects pricing strategy.

Effect of Physical Conditions on the Degree of Adaptation of the Marketing Mix in the Malaysian Export Companies

The effects of physical conditions on the likelihood to adapt the marketing strategies were tested. Physical conditions of a country encompass the geographical location, natural and artificial resources, climate, rivers, lakes, etc.

Hypothesis H8a specified that the greater the difference in physical conditions between the local and foreign markets, the greater the likelihood that exporters will adapt their product strategy. The result of the hypothesis was reported to be significant. Physical conditions that products are subjected to are likely to influence the product strategy adapted by the exporters. For example, climate difference between Malaysia and the country importing the goods is likely to cause the exporters to alter/adapt their products so that they are not affected by weather and climate change. The results obtained here are in line with findings and previous research which shows that physical conditions influence the adaptation of new product strategy. In extreme weather, foodstuffs and other perishable commodities must be protected and this will automatically result in product repackaging. It must be noted that not all factors influence the product strategy as factors such as building size; offices have no impact on the product strategy.

Hypothesis H8b specified that the difference in physical conditions between the local and foreign market, the greater the likelihood that Malaysian exporters will adapt their promotion strategy in foreign markets. The hypothesis was verified indicating that differences in the physical factors will definitely result in adaptation of promotional strategies used abroad. Most of the advertisements use the physical features that the local people can identify with and this means that great changes in the physical structures will promote the adaptation of new promotional strategies. Malaysian exporters relying on independent distributors and agents, must allow them to formulate new promotional strategies using the physical structures in the importing country.

Hypothesis H8c specified that the difference in physical conditions between the local and foreign market, the greater the likelihood that Malaysian exporters will adapt their distribution strategy in foreign markets. The hypothesis was verified indicating that physical condition differences would result in adaptation of new distribution strategies. The results are in line with Albaun, Strandskov and Duerr (2002), who found that a significant relationship exists between physical conditions and distribution strategy adaptation; but in contrast with Park (2006) who showed the reverse. Changes in the physical conditions mean that the distribution of products to the final consumer will be affected and the exporters have to identify new innovative methods to ensure the products are effectively transported to their destinations.

Hypothesis 8d specified that the difference in physical conditions between the local and foreign market, the greater the likelihood that Malaysian exporters will adapt their pricing strategy in foreign markets. This hypothesis was not verified. The results are in contradiction with what is expected as changes in other strategies are likely to affect the prices. The reason for lack of new price adaptation may be due to standardizations in the pricing strategy, such that the product has a uniform price throughout as well as reliance on foreign agents and franchises that buy from the exporters and set their own retail prices.

Effect of Marketing Infrastructure on the Degree of Adaptation of the Marketing Mix in the Malaysian Export Companies

Marketing infrastructure, as a determinant of the marketing mix adaptation, was also evaluated in this work. It was proposed that differences in the marketing infrastructure between Malaysian exporters and foreign country resulted in adaptations to the marketing mix.

Hypothesis H9a specified that the greater the difference between the marketing infrastructure of the exporters' local and foreign market, the greater the level of adaptation of the product strategy of Malaysian exporters. The hypothesis was not verified indicating that marketing infrastructure does not affect adaptation to product strategy. The main reasons that could have resulted in such inferences are standardization and harmonization of products. When products are standardized, firms find it hard to change or adapt due to the additional expenses. When adaptations are done, only trivial details such as the product packaging is changed. If the difference between the two countries is also small, firms may opt to use the same product strategy.

Hypothesis H9b specified that the greater the difference between the marketing infrastructure of the exporters' local and foreign market, the greater the level of adaptation of the promotion strategy of Malaysian exporters. The hypothesis was verified indicating that differences in the marketing infrastructure would result in adaptation of promotion strategies. This could be due to the fact that the advertising strategies used in different countries are different and this necessitates the adoption of new methods. Promotions in Malaysia, as well as the marketing methods differ, and this results in the use of different strategies.

Hypothesis H9c specified that the greater the difference between the marketing infrastructure of the exporters' local and foreign market, the greater the level of adaptation of the distribution strategy of Malaysian exporters. The hypothesis was verified meaning that marketing infrastructure changes are expected to cause changes in the distribution strategy. Changes in the marketing channels would lead to foreign companies using new distribution channels. The change may be attributed to the wide differences in the marketing infrastructure between Malaysia and importing countries.

Hypothesis H9d specified that the greater the difference between the marketing infrastructure of the exporters' local and foreign market, the greater the level of adaptation of the pricing strategy of Malaysian exporters. The hypothesis was verified indicating that differences in marketing infrastructure will result in the adoption of the foreign companies' pricing strategies. These results were obtained because changes in marketing infrastructure would lead to changes in product strategy and this would affect the final price of the product.

Impact of the Antecedent Factors on the Performance of Malaysian Export Companies through the Mediating Influence of Marketing Mix

Another objective of this study was to investigate the impact of the antecedent factors on the export performance of Malaysian export companies. It should be kept in mind that this investigation was done through the mediating impact of the marketing mix adaptation strategies. The following Table 5.2 shows the impact of antecedent factors on the export performance of Malaysian export companies through the mediating influence of marketing mix adaptation.

Impact of International Experience on the Performance of Malaysian Export Companies

Hypothesis 10.1 stated that the marketing mix adaptation mediates the effect of international experience on the performance of Malaysian export companies.

Table 5.2: The impact of antecedent factors on the performance of Malaysian export companies through the mediating influence of marketing mix adaptation

Path	*Effect*	*Path Coefficient*	*T. Statistics*	*Result*
EXP -> PER	Indirect	0.050	2.598**	Significant
TEC -> PER	Indirect	–0.021	0.488	Not Significant
COM -> PER	Indirect	–0.001	0.014	Not Significant
GOV -> PER	Indirect	–0.004	0.101	Not Significant
CUL -> PER	Indirect	0.030	0.756	Not Significant
ECO -> PER	Indirect	0.137	2.421*	Significant
IMG -> PER	Indirect	0.002	0.072	Not Significant
PHY -> PER	Indirect	0.353	5.236***	Significant
INF -> PER	Indirect	0.143	2.790**	Significant

The result of this hypothesis was reported to be significant. International experience of the firms was measured by the number of years that a company has been in operation. This experience gives firms an extra advantage as they understand the market conditions and other factors. From the results obtained, it was found that international experience affected the performance of Malaysian companies. Based on the results, it was found that experience plays a significant role in the identification of new distribution channels that would lead to increased profitability and performance of the firm. Through experience, exporting firms are able to know the right channels for distributing their products and this increases sales and profits. Greater experience in the export market also makes the firm aware of the customer's wants and needs as well as the market forces and competition. This makes export companies change/ modify their products to suit the needs of the export market which may differ from Malaysia. Therefore, international experience of a firm plays an imperative role in promoting the performance of the exporting firms.

Impact of Technology Intensity on the Performance of Malaysian Export Companies

Hypothesis 10.2 stated that the marketing mix adaptation mediates the effect of technology intensity on the performance of Malaysian export companies. The finding of this hypothesis was found to be not significant. Technology intensity or the level of technology between the firms in Malaysia and the foreign firms was investigated and the results indicated that technology intensity did not affect the performance of the Malaysian companies. This could be due to the minor technological differences that exist between Malaysia and the foreign countries that they export to. Also, standardization of products results in production of uniform products and this meant that technological changes did not give the exporters advantages over their rivals. However, in other situations, technology levels improve the performance of firms in the export industry. Improved technology promotes the production of superior products that satisfy the consumers' wants and this may promote company performance in the international market. The use of innovations and technology in management and distribution channels will lower the product costs, and this in turn can lead to increased performance.

Impact of Competition Level on the Performance of Malaysian Export Companies

Hypothesis 10.3 stated that the marketing mix adaptation mediates the effect of competition level of the industry on performance of Malaysian export companies. The result of this hypothesis was reported to be not significant. The competition level of foreign markets as compared to the Malaysian market was found to have no impact on the performance of the export market. This could be due to the fact that the competition levels in Malaysia may be similar to the exporting countries, and also the fact that most exporters rely on agents and other independent sellers. However, in markets with very high competition as opposed to the exporting country, the marketing mix must be adjusted so that the products can compete with other products.

Impact of Government Regulations on the Performance of Malaysian Export Companies

Hypothesis 10.4 stated that the marketing mix adaptation mediates the effect of differences of government regulations between home and export market on performance of Malaysian export companies. The result of this hypothesis was found to be not significant. Government regulations play an imperative role in regulating the performance of the multinational companies. Government levels of quality, taxation laws and other policies must be strictly followed. In the case of Malaysia, foreign government regulations do not significantly affect the performance of the exporters, and hence, this factor is considered trivial. This is due to the fact that most of the foreign import countries' regulations are nearly the same as those of Malaysia and this means that exporters do not have to adapt. Even though government regulations were found to have limited impacts on the performance of the exporting companies, these regulations were found to cause changes in the pricing strategy as well as the product strategy. Various researchers indicate that the legal and regulatory framework has considerable impacts on the performance of a firm at the international level. Governments may choose specific suppliers or impose exchange controls and these have direct impact on the price of the product. Exporters must adapt new marketing mix strategies in order to compete with the other firms (Beamish, 1993; Yan and Gray, 1994).

Impact of Cultural Differences on the Performance of Malaysian Export Companies

Hypothesis 10.5 stated that the marketing mix adaptation mediates the effect of cultural differences between Malaysia and export market on performance of Malaysian export companies. The result of this hypothesis was found to be not significant. Cultural differences between the exporting and importing nations play an imperative role in the determination of the performance of an exporting country. The culture, beliefs and values that people have, control their purchasing patterns. Products designated for export must be packaged and presented in a form that is culturally accepted by the local people. When there is a big cultural difference between the export and import nations, the marketing mix elements must be altered and those of the foreign nation adapted. In the case of Malaysian exporters, cultural differences between the country and the foreign nations seem small, and hence the cultural differences have no impact on the performance of the exporting companies. Since Malaysian companies rely on agents and independent distributors, they do not have to adapt or change their marketing mix as the final branding is done locally by companies in the foreign country.

Impact of Economic Differences on the Performance of Malaysian Export Companies

Hypothesis 10.6 stated that the marketing mix adaptation mediates the effect of economic differences between the exporters' home market and foreign market on performance of Malaysian export companies. The result of this hypothesis was found to be significant. Economic differences or economic distances between the exporting and importing nations have great impact on the performance of international organizations. A wide economic difference means that the two countries will have wide gap and this affects the exchange rate and prices. For example, when a developed nation sells products to a developing nation, the exchange rate may be so high that the price of the product would rise when currency conversion is done. The final price may be too high for the consumer. In the case of Malaysia, economic differences were found to have significant impacts on the willingness of the firm to adapt and the performance of the exporting company. Economic differences between the nations would trigger changes in product strategy, but all the other factors would remain unchanged.

Impact of Country Image on the Performance of Malaysian Export Companies

Hypothesis 10.7 stated that the marketing mix adaptation mediates the effect of the negative image of the exporting country (Malaysia) on performance of

Malaysian export companies. The finding of this hypothesis was reported to be not significant. The impact of country image affects the performance of international organizations in the world. For example, products from the UK and Germany are regarded as being of high quality and durable. This would affect the final price. In the study, the impact of country image on Malaysian export companies was found to have no significant impact on the performance of the companies and did not mediate in the adaptation of any marketing mix elements. This was caused by the fact that most of the importing nations have a positive attitude towards Malaysia. Also, due to the reliance on agents and other distributors, the perception that products come from Malaysia is not very high in the foreign market. For example, a company in Malaysia can identify a suitable agent with good reputation in the foreign nation, and this can boost the sales and profits. This means that the country image may be suppressed in some cases.

Impact of Physical Conditions on the Performance of Malaysian Export Companies

Hypothesis 10.8 stated that the marketing mix adaptation mediates the effect of differences in physical conditions between the exporters' home market and foreign market on performance of Malaysian export companies. The result of this hypothesis was found to be significant. The physical conditions of a given nation affect the performance of international companies. Physical conditions may increase or reduce the distribution costs and may also delay the delivery of products. In the case of Malaysia, the study indicated that physical condition differences between Malaysia and the importing nations affected the export performance by mediating in the adaptation of the foreign country's product strategy, promotion strategy and the distribution strategy. Changes in the physical conditions, such as climate differences between the exporting and importing nations, would have resulted in the need to repackage materials so as to withstand these changes. Promotional strategies had to be adapted as there were significant changes in structures and buildings and other aspects that the citizens of the foreign country adore or favour.

Impact of Marketing Infrastructure on the Performance of Malaysian Export Companies

Hypothesis 10.9 stated that the marketing mix adaptation mediates the effect of differences in marketing infrastructure between the exporters' home market and foreign market on performance of Malaysian export companies. The result of this hypothesis was found to be significant. Marketing infrastructure differences between Malaysia and other foreign nations affect the performance of the export companies. For the companies to be successful, adequate marketing must be done through the appropriate channels so as to create awareness. Changes in the marketing strategies and structures in the foreign country are likely to trigger changes in the marketing mix adapted by the exporting companies in Malaysia. The results indicated that there is a relationship between the marketing infrastructure and export performance. The main marketing mix factors that mediate the effect that marketing infrastructure has on export performance, are promotional strategies, distribution strategies and pricing strategy. Changes in promotion strategies are likely to occur if the foreign country has different marketing infrastructure and methods. The export companies must change their strategies so that it is in line with the importing nation. Also, the pricing strategy must be changed so as to reflect on the importing nations pricing. For example, if people in the foreign nation prefer to buy electronics via hire purchase instead of paying cash, the exporting companies must adjust their pricing so as to adapt to this new payment technique.

THE IMPACT OF MARKETING MIX ON THE EXPORT PERFORMANCE OF MALAYSIAN EXPORT COMPANIES

One of the objectives of the present research was to examine the influence of the marketing mix adaptation strategies on the export performance of the Malaysian export companies. Table 5.3 outlines the findings of the study regarding the direct link between the marketing mix adaptation strategies and the export performance of Malaysian export companies.

Table 5.3: The impact of marketing mix adaptation on the export performance of Malaysian export companies

Path	*Effect*	*Path Coefficient*	*T. Statistics*	*Result*
PRD -> PER	Direct	0.238	3.172**	Significant
PRM -> PER	Direct	0.224	2.971**	Significant
DIS -> PER	Direct	0.431	5.583***	Significant
PRI -> PER	Direct	–0.111	1.937	Not Significant

As can be seen in the table above, some of these links were found to be significant while others were found to be insignificant. Specifically, the direct link between the first three marketing mix strategies, namely product adaptation, promotion adaptation, and distribution adaption were found to have a significant impact on the export performance of Malaysian export companies. On the other hand, the marketing mix strategy of pricing was not found to have a significant impact on the export performance of Malaysian export companies. The following section discusses these findings.

Effect of Product Strategy on the Performance of the Malaysian Export Companies

Hypothesis 11.a stated that the greater the level of product strategy adaptation, the better the Malaysian exporters' performance. The result of this hypothesis was found to be significant. Product strategy is one of the most influential parts of the marketing mix elements. In a competitive environment, products must be differentiated from those of the competitors so as to ensure they gain competitive advantages, which also leads to branding. When products are adequately differentiated as the best quality, low priced and superior, customers will tend to buy them and this creates brand loyalty among the consumers. Product strategy is one of the key elements that affects the performance of Malaysian export companies. When products are well branded, packaged and other strategies used, the performance of the company will be enhanced. In this study, the performance of Malaysian companies was affected by the product strategy. Changes in the product strategy can be used to counter other effects and increase the performance of the company. Previous studies indicate that product strategy affects the performance of companies dealing in international trade. Research shows that companies' brand, differentiates and innovates so as to counter increased competition at the home and foreign markets (Zaiem & Zghidi, 2011 and Solberg and Durrieu, 2008). In addition to the product strategy, is product positioning where products are effectively placed so as to compete with others in the market. These modifications include packaging and labeling of the products.

Effect of Promotional Strategy on the Performance of the Malaysian Export Companies

Hypothesis 11.b stated that the greater the level of promotion strategy adaptation, the better the Malaysian exporters' performance. The result of this hypothesis was found to be significant. Promotional strategy is one of the major marketing mixes that affect the performance of firms in the export market. Studies indicate that firms need to formulate appropriate strategies so as to gain entry into the foreign market, and also to compete with the other firms in the foreign market. Firms in the foreign market dealing with the same product as the exporter have an upper hand, and hence the exporter must develop good promotional strategies to counter the effects of the competitors. In this research, it was seen that promotional strategy significantly affected the performance of the export companies. The choice of the promotional strategy depends on the differences that exist between the exporting nations and the importing nation. Exporting firms may decide to use standard promotion methods or adopt the styles that target the local consumers. The most limiting factor to adoption of varying promotion strategies at the target market is the promotional costs involved. Adaptation results in increase in marketing costs and this can only be managed by large firms who have enough human and material resources to cater for the increased costs.

Effect of Distribution Strategy on the Performance of the Malaysian Export Companies

Hypothesis 11.c stated that the greater the level of distribution strategy adaptation, the better the Malaysian exporters' performance. The result of this hypothesis was found to be significant. Another great impact on the performance of the exporting company was the distribution strategy used. The distribution method affects the efficiency of product delivery and the final pricing of the product. The use of appropriate distribution channels ensures products reach on time and at the right place. In this study, it was found that the distribution channels had a great impact on the export market. It was also found out that selection of the appropriate distribution channels was determined by the experience that the exporter had in the market (Baldauf, Cravens & Wagler, 2000). It is therefore prudent that Malaysian exporters adopt the promotional strategies used by the foreign nations. The results obtained are consistent with the finding in various studies that show that selection and proper management of the right distribution channels affect the performance of export firms. The results obtained are consistent with the findings by Monica (2006) who indicates that the distribution channels affect export performance and should be given a lot of considerations when planning the export market strategies. According to Monica (2006), the distribution strategies affect market entry success and must be continually developed overtime to ensure continued improvement of the export business.

Effect of Pricing Strategy on the Performance of the Malaysian Export Companies

Hypothesis 11.d stated that the greater the level of pricing strategy adaptation, the better the Malaysian exporters' performance. The result of this hypothesis was found to be not significant. Pricing of products also affects the performance of the exporting firms. In this research, the effects of price on the export performance were not significant indicating that it did not affect the performance of Malaysian exporters. The results obtained are in contradiction to various studies that show the changes in pricing strategies can improve the performance of a firm. Managers use different techniques during pricing and they rely on factors, such as international experience, the number of countries that the firm exports to, the physical differences between the home and foreign country, and the economic differences between the trading nations.

The results obtained in the study are consistent with some studies that show that price discrimination is becoming impossible in the modern world due to globalization. When customers discover the price variations, they can opt to buy online and ignore the exported goods. Price discrimination may also make distributors lack customers and this would result in the collapse of the distribution network (Diller & Bukhari, 1994; Myers & Harvey, 2004). Studies have also shown that standardization of products or distributors who sell similar products make it impossible to formulate different product and pricing strategies (Doole & Lowe, 2004). Standardizing is mostly used by exporters in order to maintain the brand, quality and product positioning and all these are advantages as opposed to price adaptation.

GENERAL DISCUSSION OF FINDINGS

The modern export market is filled with numerous products and services. Due to globalization, there has been an increase in trade by many international companies. This has resulted in intense competition and firms are struggling for the available market share. This has resulted in the formulation of strategies to gain a larger market share. One of the most commonly used strategies is the marketing strategy. Companies must use aggressive marketing strategies so as to gain a greater portion of the market share. Marketing strategies emphasize on the four main elements of the marketing mix, i.e., product, price, distribution and promotion. Export companies must ensure that a conclusive study is carried out so as to determine the differences that exist between the home and the foreign countries.

In this study the performance of the exporting companies in Malaysia was evaluated based on the need to change their marketing mix when they operate in a foreign land. The exporter's perception on these four main marketing mix elements was evaluated. The main aim of the study was to determine whether changes or differences between the host and foreign countries can significantly affect the current marketing mix elements and force companies to adapt. An analysis was also carried out on whether changes/ differences in physical environment, economic differences, cultural differences, technology intensity, government regulations, international experience, marketing infrastructure, country image and the competition level, affect export performance.

The findings in this research showed that some of the factors under consideration had an impact on the performance or the export of goods, while other factors had trivial effects on export performance. The main factors affecting export performance were international experience, economic differences, physical conditions and the marketing infrastructure. These factors had several mediating marketing mix strategies that needed to be adopted if there were significant differences between the home country and the foreign country The other factors did not affect the export market. The finding also shows that the main marketing mix elements that determine the market performance in Malaysia are product, distribution and promotion. The results obtained are consistent with other studies, but in some cases, the results differ considerably. The main reasons why all factors and antecedents did not affect the export market performance were that most of the countries that trade with Malaysia have a small difference in most of the factors. Another reason was the fact that most of the companies relied on distributors who formulate their own marketing mix strategies.

In addition, the results of the study were found to be consistent with the theory upon which the research is grounded. The theories upon which the study is grounded is the contingency approach and strategic-fit perspective in which the decisions made by firms whether to adapt their product, promotion, distribution or price strategies depend on the conditions and circumstances of the host markets in which it is made sure that whatever decisions made should lead to benefits to the firm and its performance. In this study, Malaysian exporting firms made decisions whether to adapt their different strategies or standardize them by making adjustment between the host market and the home market. Thus, the findings of this study reflected the theoretical grounds adopted for the study.

IMPLICATIONS OF THE STUDY

This section is divided into two main parts, the theoretical and practical implications. Both parts are presented in this research. The following section starts with the theoretical implications.

Theoretical Implications

It has been mentioned earlier that most of the research on the adaptation/standardization processes and their impact on export performance focused on two main streams. In the first stream, a number of studies investigated the impact of the antecedent factors on the overall marketing mix strategies (Park, 2006; Kim & Cavusgil, 2009). In the second stream, other research studies attempted to investigate the relationship between the marketing mix strategies and export performance (Dess, Pinkham & Yang, 2011; Tantong, Karande, Nair & Singhapakdi, 2010; Solomon, Marshall & Stuart, 2008). However, very little research attempted to explore the relationship between the antecedent factors and the export performance through the mediating influence of marketing mix strategies. In this study, the earlier two streams were examined, but more importantly, a third stream was added which is the relationship between the antecedent factors and the export performance through the mediating influence of marketing mix adaptation strategies. Most of the previous work examined the influence of the antecedent factors on the marketing mix strategies individually. In other words, the impact of each antecedent factor was examined on each of the marketing mix strategies. No studies attempted to examine the impact of the antecedent factors on the marketing mix as a whole. In this context, Lages (2001) argues that "it is necessary for marketers to develop a measure that looks into the marketing mix as a whole". This study responded to this call by dealing with the marketing mix as a whole construct.

The findings of the study showed that some marketing mix strategies do influence the relationship between the antecedent factors and export performance. Keeping in mind that this kind of link has not been thoroughly investigated in the literature, it would be highly useful for researchers to consider investigating the mediating impact of marketing mix adaptation strategies on the relationship between the antecedent factors and export performance.

This study showed that most of the marketing mix elements affected the performance of the exporting companies. From the findings, it is important to note that not all the marketing mix elements affect the performance of a company at the international level. There is therefore the need to study the market and make a correct analysis. The results also indicated that adaptations are due to differences, such as culture, competition, physical conditions, marketing infrastructure, and technology intensity, which differ from one country to another. The results obtained show that there are variations between the different regions and therefore, studies should be carried out before exporters can decide whether to adapt or standardize. Furthermore, this study also indicated that both adaptation and standardization have their advantages and disadvantages. In some cases, standardization results in higher profits, while in other cases, adaptation must be used to ensure that marketing mix is altered to enable firms to gain competitive advantage.

Practical Implications

The study has many practical implications especially to exporters operating in Malaysia. First, the main areas where the exporters should improve include international experience, economic differences, physical conditions and the marketing infrastructure. Exporters need to be aware of these factors as Malaysia and the foreign countries have differences, and this is likely to affect the performance of the company. The company needs to adapt to the foreign country's strategies so as to ensure that they remain competitive in the market. The results can be used by managers to evaluate the physical, economic and other factors that are imperative in the export market. The report can be a guide for managers during decision making as they will be able to know the main factors to consider when making the adaptation plan. Using this report, managers will be able to know whether to adapt or standardize their marketing mix elements.

This report is also important to the policy makers in Malaysia. Using the results obtained, the main factors causing huge differences between Malaysia and the foreign country can be identified. This means that policy makers can try to bridge the gap between the two nations so as to make it easy for more export activities.

The results are also useful to the academic fraternity who can use them to determine the effects of each factor and perhaps, this will shed light that not all factors mediate in the export performance.

Finally, it has been mentioned earlier in the first chapter that the findings of the study are hoped to benefit other countries, emerging countries in particular such as Saudi Arabia. So, one of the practical recommendations of the current study is to other emerging countries such as Saudi Arabia to benefit from the findings of this study by adopting the best adaptation strategies, particularly when the items being produced and exported are similar to the items that have been used in this study. This attempt would lead to a better exporting performance and thus a better economy.

STUDY LIMITATIONS

Though the present research provides useful and interesting information, it is not without its limitations. Just like all research, this study has some weaknesses and the above conclusions and contributions should be considered in the light of these limitations. First, the present research was conducted on a specific region, namely Malaysia, and the results obtained might not be applicable in other countries and regions. Second, future researchers who consider conducting similar studies should keep in mind that the data collection phase is time and effort consuming. In the present research, data collection extended for more than four months, with the help of a number of enumerators who are experts in the field. This is because it was difficult at times to find the respondents and to get an appointment. Furthermore, some respondents were not very cooperative in the email questionnaires and it took several reminders to finally get the responses.

RECOMMENDATIONS

Based on the findings that have been generated in the present research, a number of recommendations are provided:

- The exporters need to carefully evaluate the market and adapt new strategies in the countries where there are significant differences in international experience, physical conditions and marketing infrastructure.
- The choice of a company to adapt or standardize their operations should only be done after a thorough market survey as some areas may not need adaptations due to differences in cultural, social and economic factors.
- Malaysian exporters need to use these finding to improve their services and export products.

RECOMMENDATIONS FOR FUTURE RESEARCH

First and foremost, the current research dwelt on specific region and the results obtained are for Malaysia. There is a need to replicate this study in other countries so as to determine whether the same antecedents apply.

Secondly, these results generated might not be conclusive as there is no comparative analysis with another country. In future, it is also recommended that a comparative analysis of Malaysia and other countries be done. In such a study, the differences that lead to adaptation can be checked and compared to those of Malaysia.

Thirdly, a more holistic construction of a questionnaire for the future studies needs to be developed. The questionnaire should not only ask about the tendency to adapt new strategies but also prompt managers to explain why they would not change adapt in case of wide differences in cultural, economic, technological factors, etc.

References

Aaby, N.E. and S.F. Slater (1989). "Management Influences on Export Performance: A Review of the Empirical Literature 1978-88," *International Marketing Review*, 6 (4), pp. 7-2ES6.

Abdul Adis, A. and Md. Sidin, S. (2010). "Export performance on the Malaysian wooden furniture industry: An empirical study". *Journal of International Food and Agribusiness Marketing*, 22(1&2), 52-69.

Adis, A. (2010). "Export Performance on the Malaysian Wooden Furniture Industry: An Empirical Study". *Journal of International Food and Agribusiness Marketing*, 22(1/2), 52-69.

Ahlstrom, D. and Bruton, G.D. (2010). International management: Strategy and Culture in the Emerging World. Australia: South-Western Cengage Learning.

Ahmed, S. and Rock, J. (2012). Exploring the Relationship between Export Intensity and Exporter. Characteristics, Resources, and Capabilities: Evidence from Chile. *Latin American Business Review* 13(1), 29-57.

Akaah, I.P. (1991). "Strategy Standardization in International Marketing: An Empirical Investigation of its degree of Use and Correlates", *Journal of Global Marketing*, 4(2), pp. 39-62.

Albaum, G., Strandskov, J., and Duerr, E. (2002). *International marketing and export management*. Harlow, England: Pearson Education.

—— and Tse, D.K. (2001). "Adaptation of International Marketing Strategy Components, Competitive Advantage, and Firm's Performance: A Study of Hong Kong Exporters", *Journal of International Marketing*, 9(4), pp. 59-81.

Aldrich, H.E. (1979). *Organizations and Environments*. Englewood Cliffs, NJ: Prentice-Hall.

Alvi, F. (2012). "Rethinking the institutional contexts of emerging markets through metaphor analysis". *Management International Review*, 52(4), 519-539.

Antonio, K.W.L., Yam, R.C.M., and Esther Tang, E. (2007). "The Impacts of Product Modularity on Competitive Capabilities and Performance: An Empirical Study", *International Journal of Production Economics*, Volume 105, Issue 1, pp. 1-20.

Armstrong, J.S., and Overton, T.S. (1977). "Estimating Nonresponse Bias in Mail.

Aviv, S., Makovec, B.M., Vesna, V. and Ayalla, R. (2008). "International Standardization of Channel Management and Its Behavioral and Performance Outcomes". *Journal of International Marketing*, 16(2), 120-151.

Aybar, C.B. (2012). "Corporate Governance and Firm Value in Emerging Markets: An Empirical Analysis of ADR Issuing Emerging Market Firms". *Emerging Markets Journal*, 2, 37-51.

Aydin, N. and Terpstra, V. (1981). "Marketing Know-How Transfers By Multinationals: A Case Study in Turkey", *Journal of International Business Studies*, 12(3), pp. 35-48.

Baalbaki, I.B. and Malhotra, N.K. (1993). "Marketing Management Bases For International Market Segment: An Alternate Look At The Standardization/Customization Debate", *International Marketing Review*, 10(1), pp. 19-43.

Bagozzi, R.P., and Yi, Y. (1988). "On the Evaluation of Structural Equation Models", *Journal of the Academy of Marketing Science*. 16, Number. 1, pp. 74-94.

Bain, (1968). Industrial organization (Economic theory); Industries; Industrial policy; 2nd edition United States.

Baldauf, A., Cravens, D.W. and Wagner, U. (2000). "Examining determinants of export performance in small open economies", *Journal of World Business*, 35(1): 61-79.

Barker, A.T. (1993). "A Marketing Oriented Perspective of Standardized Global Marketing", *Journal of Global Marketing*, 7(2), pp. 123-130.

—— and Aydin, N. (1991). "Implications of Standardization in Global Markets", *Journal of International Consumer Marketing*, 3(4), pp. 15-34.

Barney, J.B. (1991). "Firm resources and sustainable competitive advantage". *Journal of Management,* 17 (1), pp. 99 120.

——; Wright, M.; Ketchen Jr., D.J. (2001). "The resource-based view of the firm: Ten years after 1991". *Journal of Management*; 27 (6), pp. 625-641.

Beamish, P.W. (2000). *Asia-pacific Cases in Strategic Management.* USA: McGraw-Hill

Benson, J.D. (2009). "The Relationship between Emotional Intelligence and Managers' Use of Specific Directive and Supportive Behaviors", Unpublished dissertation presented in partial fulfillment of the requirements for the degree doctor of management in organizational leadership, University of Phoenix.

Boddewyn, J.J. and Grosse, R. (1995). "American Marketing in the European Union: Standardization's Uneven Progress (1973-1993)", *European Journal of Marketing*, 29(12), pp. 23-42.

——, Soehl, R. and Picard, J. (1986). "Standardization of International Marketing: Is Ted Levitt in Fact Right?" *Business Horizons*, 29 (November-December), pp. 69-75.

Bradley, F. (2002). "A synthesis of cultural influence on buyer behavior", *International Marketing Strategy* 4th edition, United Kingdom: Pearson Education.

Brei, V.A., D'Avila, L., Camargo, L.F. and Engels, J. (2011). "The influence of adaptation and standardization of the marketing mix on performance: A meta-analysis". *Brazilian Administration Review*, 8(3).

Burns, T. and Stalker, G.M. (1967). "The Management of Innovation", Tavistok: London.

Buzzell, R.D. (1968). "Can you Standardize Multinational Marketing?", *Harvard Business Review*, 46(6), pp. 102-113.

Calantone, Roger, J.; Kim, Daekwan.; Schmidt, Jeffrey, B.; and Cavusgil, S. Tamer. (2006). "The Influence of Internal and External Firms Factors on International Product Adaptation Strategy and Export Performance: A Three-Country Comparison", *Journal of Business Research*, 59, pp. 176-185.

——; Cavusgil, S. Tamer; Schmidt, Jeffrey, B.; and Shin, Geon-Cheol (2004). "Internationalization and the Dynamics of Product Adaptation: An Empirical Investigation", *Product Innovation Management*, 21, pp. 185-198.

Carlos M.P. Sousa and Frank Bradley (2008). Price adaptation in export markets. Marketing Group, UCD Michael Smurfit School of Business, University College Dublin, Dublin, Ireland.

Carpano, Claudio and Chrisman, James J.(1995). "Performance Implications of

International Product Strategies and the Integration of Marketing Activities," *Journal of International Marketing*, Vol. 3(1), 1995, 9-27.

Cavana, R.Y., Delahaye, B.L. and Sekaran, U. (2001). *Applied business research.*

Cavusgil, S.T. and Michigan State University. (2009). Michigan State University contributions to international business and innovation. Bingley: JAI Press.

—— and Kirpalani, V.H. (1993). "Introducing Products into Export Markets: Success Factors", *Journal of Business Research*, 27(1/2): 1-15.

—— and Zou, S. (1994). "Marketing Strategy Performance Relationship: An Investigation of the Empirical Link in Export Market Ventures", *Journal of Marketing*, 58 (1), pp. 1-21.

——, and Naidu, G.M. (1993). "Product and Promotion Adaptation in Export Venture: An Empirical Investigation", *Journal of International Business Studies*, 24 (3), pp. 479-505.

Chandran, VGR. and Veera P. (2003). "Export Specialization, Concentration and Intra-Industry Trade: Evidence from Malaysia". *Journal Akademik*, Issue 3. October, pp. 99 111.

Chattopadhyay, A., Batra, R. and Ozsomer, A. (2012). *The new emerging market.*

Chen, Z.X., Tsui, A.S. and Farh, J.L. (2002). "Loyalty to Supervisor vs. Organizational Commitment: Relationships to Employee Performance in China", *Journal of Occupational and Organizational Psychology*, Vol. 75, pp. 339-356.

Chetty, S.K. and Hamilton, R.T. (1993). "Firm-level Determinant of Export Performance: A Meta-analysis", *International Marketing Review*, 10(3), pp. 26-34.

Chorn, N.H. (1991). "The Alignment Theory: Creating Strategic Fit", *Management Decision*, 29 (1), pp. 20-26.

Christensen, C.H.; Da Rocha, A. and Gertner, R.K. (1987). "An empirical Investigation of the Factors Influencing Exporting success of Brazilians Firms", *Journal of International Business Studies*, 18(3), pp. 61-77.

Chung, H.F.L. (2004). "An Empirical Investigation of Immigrant Effects: The Experience of Firms Operating in the Emerging Market," *International Business Review*, 13(6), pp. 705-28.

—— and Enderwick, P. (2003). "An Investigation of Market Entry Strategy Selection: Exporting vs Foreign Direct Investment Modes—A Home-Host Country Scenario," *Asia Pacific Journal of Management*, 18(4), pp. 443-60.

—— (2002). "An Empirical Investigation of Marketing Programme and process Elements in the Host-Home Scenario", *Journal of Global Marketing*, 16(1), pp. 141 186.

—— (2005). "An Investigation of Cross-Market Standardization Strategies—Experiences in the European Union", *European Journal of Marketing*, 39 (11-12), pp. 1345-1371.

—— (2007). "International Marketing Standardization Strategies Analysis: A Cross-National Investigation", *Asia Pacific Journal of Marketing and Logistics*, 19(2), pp. 145-167.

—— (2009). "Structure of Marketing Decision Making and International Marketing Standardization Strategies", *European Journal of Marketing*, 43 (5/6), pp. 794-825.

Cohen, W. and Levinthal, D. (1990). "Absorptive Capacity: A New Perspective on Learning and Innovation". *Administrative Science Quarterly*, 35: 128-152.

Cooper, Robert G. and Kleinschmidt, Elko J. (1985). "The Impact of Export Strategy on Export Sales Performance". *Journal of International Business Studies*, 18 (Spring), pp. 37-55.

Culpan, R. (1989). "Export Behavior of Firms: Relevance of Firm Size", *Journal of Business Research,* 18, pp. 207-218.

Czinkota, M.R., and Ronkainen, I.A. (1990). *International Marketing* (2nd ed.). Chicago: The Dryden Press.

Czinkota, M. Ronkainen, I. (2007). *International Marketing* 8th edition, USA: Thomson

Da Rocha A., Christensen C.H., Da Cunha CE. (1990). "Aggressive and Passive Exporters: A Study In The Brazilian Furniture Industry". *International Marketing Review*, 7(5), pp. 6-15.

—— (1994). "The Export Experience of a Developing Country: a Review of Empirical Studies of Export Behavior And the Performance of Brazilian Firms". In: Tamer Cavusgil S., Axinn C., editors. *Advances in International Marketing*. New York.

Daub, M. (2009). *Coordination of service Off shoring subsidiaries in multinational corporations*. Wiesbaden: Gabler.

De Luz, M. (1993). "Relationship between Export Strategy variables and Export Performance for Brazil-based Manufacturers", *Journal of Global Marketing*, 7(1), pp. 87-110.

Dekkers, R. (2009). *Dispersed manufacturing networks: Challenges for research and practice*. Dordrecht: Springer.

Dess, G.G., Pinkham, B.C. and Yang, H. (2011). "Entrepreneurial Orientation: Assessing the Construct's Validity and Addressing Some of Its Implications for Research in the Areas of Family Business and Organizational Learning". *Entrepreneurship Theory and Practice*, 35(5), 1077-1090.

——, G.T. Lumpkin, and Jeffrey G. Covin. (1997). "Entrepreneurial Strategy Making and Firm Performance: Tests of Contingency and Configurational Models." *Strategic Management Journal*, 18(9), pp. 677-695.

Devinney, T.M., Pedersen, T. and Tihanyi, L. (2010). "The past, present and future of international business and management". Bingley: Emerald.

Dichtl E., Koglmayr H., Muller S. (1990). "International orientation as a precondition for export success". *Journal of International* Business Studies, 21(Spring), pp. 23-40.

Diller, H. and Bukhari, I. (1994). "Pricing Conditions in the European Common Market". *European Management Journal*, 12 (2): 163-170.

Doole, I. and Lowe, R. (2004). "International Marketing Strategy: Analysis, Development and Implementation". London: Thomson Learning.

—— (2008). International marketing strategy: Analysis, development and implementation. London: Cengage Learning.

Douglas, S.P., and Craig, C.S. (1986). "Global marketing myopia". *Journal of Marketing Management*, 2(2), 155-169.

——, and Wind, Y. (1987). "The Myth of Globalization". *Columbia Journal of World Business*, 22(4), 19-29.

——, and Samuel C. Craig (1989). "Evolution of Global Marketing Strategy: Scale, Scope and Synergy," *Columbia Journal of World Business*, 24 (Fall), pp. 47-59.

Drazin, R. and Van de Ven, A.H. (1985). "Alternative Forms of Fit in Contingency Theory." *Administrative Science Quarterly*, 30, pp. 514-539.

Enderwick, P. (2009). *Responding to global crisis: The contribution of emerging markets*.

Eusebio, R., Andreu, J.L., and Belbeze, M.P.L. (2007). Management perception and marketing strategy in export performance. *Journal of fashion marketing and management,* 11, (1), 24-40. Export performance: A review of the research in the literature between 1998 and 2005, *International Journal of Management Review*, Vol. 10, No. 4, pp. 343-374.

Ford, D. and Leonidou, L. (1991). "Research Developments In International Marketing: A European Perspective", in Paliwoda, S.J., (ed.) *New Perspectives on International Marketing* (London: Routledge), pp. 3-32.

Fornell, C., and Larcker, D.F. (1981). "Evaluating Structural Equation Models with Unobservable Variables and Measurement Error", *Journal of Marketing Research*, 18, pp. 39-50.

Freeman, J., Styles, C. and Lawley, M. (2012). "Does firm location make a difference to the export performance of SMEs?" *International Marketing Review* 29(1), 88-113.

Galbraith, J.R., and Kazanjian, R.K. (1986). *Strategy implementation: Structure, systems and process* (2nd ed.). St. Paul: West.

Gerpott, T.J. and Jakopin, N.M. (2005). "International Marketing Standardization and Financial Performance of Mobile Network Operators-An Empirical Analysis", *Schmalenbach Business Review*, 57(3), pp. 198-228.

Govindarajan, V. (1988). "A Contingency Approach to Strategy Implementation at the Business-unit Level: Integrating Administrative Mechanisms with Strategy", *Academy of Management Journal*, 31 (4), pp. 826-853.

H. Wold. (1982). "Soft modeling: The basic design and some extensions". In J.K. J¨oreskog and H. Wold, editor, *Systems Under Indirect Observation*, volume 2, pages 1-53. North Holland, Amsterdam.

—— (1985). "Partial least squares". In S. Kotz and N.L. Johnson, editors, *Encyclopedia of the Statistical Sciences*, volume 6, pages 581-591. John Wiley & Sons.

Habib, M.M. and B. Victor (1991). "Strategy Structure and Performance of U.S. Manufacturing And Service MNCs: A Comparative Analysis," *Strategic Management Journal*, 12, pp. 589-606.

Hamel, G. and Prahalad, C.K. (1985). "Do you Really Have a Global Strategy?". *Harvard Business Review*, July-August, pp. 139-48.

Han, C.M. and Kim, J.M. (2003). "Korean Marketing in China: An Exploratory Analysis of Strategy-Performance Relationships", *Journal of International Marketing*, 11(2), pp. 79-100.

Harvey, M.G. (1993). "Point of View: A Model to Determine Standardization of the Advertising Process in International Markets". *Journal of Advertising Research*, 33 (4), pp. 57-64.

He, X. and Wei, Y. (2011). "Linking market orientation to international market selection and international performance". *International Business Review* 20(5), 535-546.

Hien, H.L.P. (2010). "The Study of Relationship between Salesperson Behaviors, Trust, Customer Equity and Loyalty Intentions", Unpublished thesis submitted in partial of requirements for the degree of Master of business administration, Southern Taiwan University.

Hieu, H. and Truong, Q. (2010). "Internationalization and its impacts on the standardization/adaptation mode of operations: A study of two Italian firms in Vietnam". *Asia Pacific Business Review*, 16(1-2), 239-257.

Hill, J.S. and Still, R.R. (1984). "Adapting Products to LDC Tastes", *Harvard Business Review*, 62(2), pp. 92-101.

Hise, R., (2010). "Are US companies employing standardization or adaptation strategies in their international markets?" *Journal of International Business and Cultural Studies*, 41-29.

Hoskisson, R.E., and Hoskisson, R.E. (2008). *Competing for advantage*. Mason, OH: Thomson/South-Western.

Hout, T., Porter, M.E. and Rudden, E. (1982). "How Global Companies Win Out?". *Harvard Business Review*, 60 (3), pp. 70-79.

http://www.fmm.org.my/About_FMM-@-Contact_Us.aspx

http://www.matrade.gov.my/en/contents-section/55-publications/384-annual-reports

J. Nilsson, S. de Jong, and A.K. Smilde. (1997). Multiway Calibration in 3D QSAR.

J.S. Hulland (1999). "Use of partial least squares (PLS) in strategic management research: A review of four recent studies". *Strategic Management Journal*, 20: 195-204.

Jain, S.C., and Griffith, D.A. (2011). *Handbook of research in international marketing.* Cheltenham, UK: Edward Elgar.

—— (1989). "Standardization of International Marketing Strategy: Some Research Hypothesis", *Journal of Marketing*, 53(1), pp. 70-79.

Jatusripitak, S., Fahey, L., and Kotler, P. (1985). "Strategic global marketing: Lessons from the Japanese". *Columbia Journal of World Business*, 20(2), 47-53.

Javalgi, R.R.G. and Todd, P.R. (2011). "Entrepreneurial orientation, management commitment, and human capital: The internationalization of SMEs in India", *Journal of Business Research*, 64(9), 1004-1010.

Jeannet, J.P. and Hennessey, H.D. (2001). "*Global Marketing Strategies*", 5th Edition, Boston: Houghton Mifflin.

Johnson, J.L. and Arunthanes, W. (1995). "Ideal and Actual Product Adaptation in US Exporting Firms", *International Marketing Review*, 12(3), pp. 3-46.

Julian, C.C. (2003). "Export marketing performance: A study of Thailand firms". *Journal of small business management*, 41, (2), 213-221.

K.J. Worsley. (1997). "An overview and some new developments in the statistical analysis of PET and fMRI data". *Human Brain Mapping*, 5: 254-258.

Kacker, M.P. (1975). "Export-oriented product adaptation—its patterns and problems", *Management International Review*, 16(1), pp. 61-70.

Katsikeas, C.S., Leonidas, S., Leonidou, C. and Morgan, N.A. (2000). "Firm-level export performance assessment: review, evaluation, and development", *Journal of the Academy of Marketing Science*, 28 (4), pp. 493-511.

——, Samiee, S. and Theodosiou, M. (2006). "Strategy Fit and Performance Consequences of International Marketing Standardization". *Strategic Management Journal*, 27 (9), pp. 867-890.

Kaufmann, L. and Roesch, J. (2012). "Constraints to Building and Deploying Marketing Capabilities by Emerging Market Firms in Advanced Markets". *Journal of International Marketing*, 20(4), 1-24.

Keats, B.W. and Hitt, M.A. (1988). "A Causal Model of Linkages among Environmental Dimensions, Macro Organizational Characteristics and Performance", *Academy of Management Journal*, 31 (3), pp. 570-598.

Keegan, W.J. (1969). "Multinational Product Planning: Strategic Alternatives", *Journal of Marketing*, January, pp. 58-62.

Kiss, A.N., Danis, W.M. and Cavusgil, S.T. (2011). "International entrepreneurship research in emerging economies: A critical review and research agenda". *Journal of Business Venturing*, 1, 266-290.

Koh, A.C. and Robicheaux, R.A. (1988). "Variations in Export Performance Due to Differences in Export Marketing Strategy: Implications for Industrial Marketers", *Journal of Business Research*, 17(3), pp. 249-258.

Kostova, T., Roth K. and Dacin M.T. (2008). "Institutional theory in the study of multinational corporations: A critique and new directions". *Academy of Management Review* 33(4), 994-1006.

Kotabe, M. and Helsen, K. (2009). *The SAGE handbook of international marketing*. Los Angeles: SAGE.

Kotler, Philip (1986). "Global Standardization—Courting Danger". *Journal of Consumer Marketing*, 3 (Spring), pp. 13-15.

Kustin, R.A. (2010). "Performance and standardization of Australian, Japanese and US firms". *Asia Pacific Journal of Marketing and Logistics*, 22(4), 447-459.

Lages, L.F., Jap S.D., and Griffith, D.A. (2008). "The Role of Past Performance In Export Ventures: A Short-Term Reactive Approach". *Journal of International Business Studies*, 39, pp. 304-325.

—— and Montgomery, D.B. (2001). "The effects of Prior Export Performance on Firm's Commitment to Exporting and Marketing Strategy Adaptation to the Foreign Market: Evidence from Small and Medium-sized Exporters", Research Paper No. 1701. Stanford University: Graduate School of Business.

——, and Lages, C.R. (2004). "The STEP scale: A measure of short-term export performance improvement". *Journal of international marketing*, 12(1), 36-56.

——, Silva, G., and Styles, C., (2009). "Relationship capabilities, quality, and innovation as determinants of export performance". *Journal of international marketing*, 17(4), 47-70.

Lages, L.P., José, L.A. and Cristiana, R.L. (2008). "The STRATADAPT scale: A measure of marketing strategy adaptation to international business markets". *International Marketing Review*, 25(5), 584-600.

Lawrence, P.R. and Lorsch, J.W. (1967). *Organization and Environment: Managing Differentiation and Integration*, Harvard University Press: Boston, MA.

Lee, C. and Griffith, D.A. (2004). "The marketing strategy-performance relationship in an export-driven developing economy". *Journal of international marketing Review*, 21 (3), 321-334.

Leonidou, L.C. and Katsikeas, C.S. and Samiee, S. (2002). Marketing Strategy determinates of export performance: A meta-analysis. *Journal of Business research*. 55, (1), 517 567.

Levitt, T. (1983). "The Globalization of Markets," *Harvard Business Review*, 61(3),

Luo, Y., Liu, Y. and Xue, J. (2009). "Relationship investment and channel performance: An analysis of mediating forces". *Journal of Management Studies*, 46, 1113-1137.

M. Martens and H. Martens. (1986). "Partial Least Squares Regression". In J.R. Piggott, editor, *Statistical Procedures in Food Research*, pp. 293-359. Elsevier Applied Science, London. D.V. Nguyen and D.M. Rocke. (2002). Tumor classification by partial least squares using microarray gene expression data. Bioinformatics, 18: 39-50.

Madsen, T.K. (1987). "Successful Export Marketing Management: Some Empirical Evidence", *International Marketing Review*, 6, (4).

Maheran, M. (2008). "Export Competitiveness of Malaysian Electrical and Electronic (E&E) Product: Comparative Study of China, Indonesia and Thailand". *International Journal of Business and Management.*

Manolova, T.S., Brush, C.G., and Edelman, L.F. (2008). "What Do Women Entrepreneurs Want", *Strategic Change*, 17, pp. 69-82.

Mavrogiannis, M., Bourlakis, M.A., Dawson, P.J., and Mitchell, R.N. (2008). "Assessing export performance in the Greek food and beverage industry". *Journal of British food.* 110 (7), 638-654.

Mesquita, L.F. and Lazzarini, S.G. (2008). "Horizontal and vertical relationships in developing economies: implications for SMEs' access to global markets". *Academy of Management Journal*, 51, 359-380.

Miles, R.E., and Snow, C.C. (1989). *Organizational Strategy, Structure, and Process.* New York: McGraw-Hill.

Monica, G. (2006). *Export Marketing Strategies for High Performance: Evidence from Spanish Exporting Companies*. San Francisco State University.

Morgan, A.N., Kaleka, A., and Katsikeas, S.C. (2004). "Antecedent of export venture performance: A theoretical model and empirical assessment". *Journal of marketing*, 68(1), 90-108.

Myers, M. and M. Harvey (2004). "The Value of Pricing Control in Export Channels: A Governance Perspective", *Journal of International Marketing*, 9 (4). Reprinted in: International Marketing, S. Paliwoda & J. Ryans (Eds.) E. Edgar, Cheltenham Glos, UK. 2006.

N.J. Lobaugh, R. West, and A.R. McIntosh. (2001). "Spatiotemporal analysis of experimental differences in event-related potential data with partial least squares". *Psychophysiology*, 38: 517-530.

Nadler, D.A. and Tushman, M.L. (1979). "A congruence model for diagnosing organizational behavior". In D. Kolb, I. Rubin and J. McIntyre. Organisational Psychology: A book of Readings. (3rd ed). Englewood Cliffs, N.J.: Prentice Hall.

Naman, J.L., and Slevin, D.P. (1993). "Entrepreneurship and the Concept of Fit: A Model and Empirical Tests". *Strategic Management Journal*, 14, 137-153.

Nassimbeni, G. (2001). "Technology, innovation capacity, and the export attitude of small manufacturing firms". *Journal of research policy*, 30 (2), 245-262.

Nigam, R. and Su, Z. (2010). "Climbing up the Performance Ladder: A Conceptual Framework for Emerging Country Multinationals". *International Journal of Business and Management*, 5 (4), 13-25.

O'Cass, A. and Julian, C. (2003). "Examining Firm and Environmental Influences on Export Marketing Mix Strategy and Export Performance of Australian Exporters", *European Journal of Marketing*, 37(3/4), pp. 366-284. offshoring. Basingstoke, Hampshire: New York.

Ogunmokun, G., Ng, S. (2004). "Factors influencing export performance in international marketing: A study of Australian firms". *International journal of management*. 21, (2), 56-69.

Ohmae, K. (1985). *Triad power: The Coming Shape of Global Competition*. New York: The Free Press.

Onkvizit, S. and Shaw J.J. (1990). "Global Advertising: Revolution or Myopia". *Journal of Organization Across Nation, USA:* Sage Publication International Consumer Marketing, 2 (3), pp. 97-112.

Oshri, I., Kotlarsky, J. and Willcocks, L. (2009). The handbook of global outsourcing and

Özsomer, A. and Simonin, B.L. (2004). "Marketing Program Standardization: A Cross-Country Exploration". *International Journal of Research in Marketing*, 21, pp. 397-419.

Park, S.I. (2006). An Empirical Investigation of the Marketing Program Adaptation of Korean Exporters, Unpublished Dissertation, George Washington University.

Peebles, D.M., and Ryans, J.K., Jr. (1984). "Management of International Advertising: A Marketing Approach". Boston: Allyn and Bacon.

Peng, M.W. (2009). Global strategy. Mason, Ohio: South-Western/Cengage Learning.

—— (2011). Global business. Mason, OH: South Western Cengage Learning.

Powers, T.L. and Loyka, J.J. (2010). "Adaptation of Marketing Mix Elements in International Markets". *Journal of Global Marketing*, 23(1), 65-79.

Pudelko, M. and Harzing, A. (2008). "The Golden Triangle for MNCs: Standardization Towards Headquarters Practices, Standardization towards Global Best Practices and Localization". *Organizational Dynamics*, 37(4), 394-404.

Quelch, John A. and Hoff, Edward J. (1986). "Customizing Global Marketing". *Harvard Business Review*, 64(May-June), pp. 59-68.

Rau, P.A. and Preble, J.F. (1987). "Standardization of Marketing Strategy by Multinationals". *International Marketing Review*, 4 (3), pp. 18-28. *Review*, 14(2), pp. 107-123.

Robles, F. and Akhter, S.H. (1997). "International Catalog Mix Adaptation: An Empirical Study", *Journal of Global Marketing*, 11 (2), pp. 65-91.

Rocha, T.V. and Silva, S.C. (2011). The adaptation versus standardization dilemma: the case of an American company in brazil. *Internext—Revista Eletrônica de Negócios Internacionais da ESPM, São Paulo*, 6(1), 63-83.

Rosenbloom, B. and Larsen, T.L. (1991). "International Channels and Distribution and the Role of Marketing Comparative Analysis", *Journal of Global Marketing*, 4(4), pp. 39-54.

Ryans, J., Griffith, D. and Jain, S. (2008). *A historical examination of the evolution of international advertising standardization/adaptation thought*. 1, 279-293.

S. Wold, H. Ruhe, H. Wold, and W.J. Dunn III. (1984). "The collinearity problem in linear regression. The partial least squares (PLS) approach to generalized inverse". *SIAM Journal of Scientific and Statistical Computations*, 5: 735-743.

Sahar-Khiz, A. (2010). "An Exploratory Examination of Relationships between Project Managers' Emotional Intelligence and Personality Styles", Unpublished dissertation presented in Partial Fulfillment of the Requirements for the Degree of Doctor of Philosophy, *Applied Management and Decision Sciences*, Walden University.

Salavou, H.E. and Halikias, J. (2008). "Strategy types of exporting firms: A view on the basis of competitive advantage". *European Business Review of Journal*, 21(2), 144-158.

Samiee, S. (1993). "Retailing and Channel Considerations in Developing Countries: A Review and Research Propositions", 27 (12), pp. 48-66.

Saudi Chamber of Commerce, (2012). fourth Edition.

Saunders, M., Lewis, P., and Thornhill, A. (2003). "Research Methods for Business Students", 3rd Edition, *Financial Times* Prentice-Hall, London.

Schilke, M.R. and Thomas, J. (2009). "When Does International Marketing Standardization Matter to Firm Performance?" *Journal of International Marketing*, 17(4), 24-46.

Sekaran, U. (2003). *Research methods for business* (4th ed.). Hoboken, NJ: John Wiley & Sons.

Sethi, S.P. (1971). "Comparative Cluster Analysis for World Markets", *Journal of Marketing Research*, 8, pp. 348-354.

Shazali Abu Mansor and Alias Radam (2000). ASEAN Industrial Cooperation and Intra ASEAN Trade: The Malaysian Case, Working Paper 9, University Putra Malaysia.

Sheth, J.N. (2011). "Impact of Emerging Markets on Marketing: Rethinking Existing Perspectives and Practices." *Journal of Marketing*, 75(4), 166-182.

Shoham A. (2002). "Export performance and market orientation: establishing an empirical link". *Journal of Business Research*, 55(3), pp. 217- 2.

—— (1995). "Global Marketing Standardization", *Journal of Global Marketing*, 9(1/2), pp. 91-119.

—— (1999). "Bounded Rationality, Planning, Standardization of International Strategy and Export Performance: A Structural Model Examination", *Journal of International Marketing*, 7(2), pp. 24-50.

—— (1996). "Marketing Mix Standardization: Determinants of Export Performance", *Journal of Global Marketing*, 10(2), pp. 53-73.

Solberg, C.A., and Durrieu, F. (2008). "Strategy Development in International Markets: A Two Tier Approach." *International Marketing Review*, 25(5), 520-543.

Solomon, M.R., Marshall, G.W. and Stuart, E.W. (2008). Marketing—Real people, real choices, Upper Saddle River, New Jersey: Pearson education, Inc.

Sorenson, Ralph Z. and Wiechmann, Ulrich E. (1975). "How Multinationals View Marketing Standardization". *Harvard Business Review*, 53(May-June), pp. 38-54.

Sousa, C.M. P., Martinez-Lopez, F.J., and Coelho, F. (2008). "The determinants of

—— and Lengler, J. (2009). Psychic distance, marketing strategy and performance in export ventures of Brazilian firms. *Journal of Marketing Management*, 25(5/6): 591-610.

—— and Bradley, F. (2008). "Antecedents of International Pricing Adaptation and Export Performance". *Journal of World Business*, 43 (3), pp. 307-320.

Stefan, S. and Thomas, K. (2011). 50 years of research on international standardization and adaptation—From a systematic literature analysis to a theoretical framework. *International Business Review*, 20(5), 491-507.

Stewart, D.B. and McAuley, A. (2000). "Congruence of Domestic and Export Marketing Strategies—An Empirical Investigation of Its Performance Implications", *International Marketing Review*, 17(6), pp. 563-586.

Stimpert, J. and I. Duhaime (1997). "In the eyes of the beholder: conceptualizations of relatedness held by the managers of large diversified firms", *Strategic Management Journal*, 18, pp. 111-125.

Style, C., and Ambler, T. (2000). "The impact of relational variable on export performance: An empirical investigation in Australia and the UK". *Australian Journal of Management*, 25(2), 261-281. Surveys, *Journal of Marketing Research* (14), pp. 396-402.

Tan, J. and Litschert, R.J., (1994). "Environment-strategy relationship and its performance implications: An empirical study of Chinese electronics industry". *Strategic Management Journal*, 15, pp. 1-20.

Tantong, P., Karande, K., Nair, A. and Singhapakdi, A. (2010). "The Effect of product adaptation and market orientation on export performance: A survey of Thai managers". *Journal of Marketing Theory and Practice*, 18(2), 155-170.

Terpstra, V. and R. Sarathy (2000). *International Marketing*. Forth Worth, TX: The Dryden Press.

—— (1987). *International Marketing*, Chicago: Dryden Press.

Theodosiou, M. and Leonidou, L.C. (2003). "Standardization versus Adaptation of International Marketing Strategy: An Integrative Assessment of the Empirical Research", *International Business Review*, 12(2), pp. 141-71.

Thirkell, P.C. and Dau, R. (1998). "Export performance: Success determinants for New Zealand Manufacturing exporters". *European Journal of marketing*, 32, (9/10), 813-829.

Toyne, B. and Walters, P.C.P. (1989). *Global Marketing Management: A Strategic Perspective*. Boston: Allyn and Bacon.

UNCTAD Report (2006). Report on FDI Inflows To South, East, And South-East Asia Achieve New High, released at press conference on 16 October, 2006, UNCTAD/PRESS/PR/2006/031, http://www.unctad.org/Templates/webflyer.asp?docid = 7463&intItemID = 3642&lang = 1 accessed on March 15th, 2010.

UNCTAD Report, (2008). Report on Globalization Facts and Figures released at press conference on 22 April, 2008, UNCTAD/PRESS/PR/Accra/2008/024, 22/04/08 http://www.unctad.org/TEMPLATES/Webflyer.asp?docID = 10072&intItemID = 1528&lang = 1 accessed on November 19th, 2009.

UNCTAD Report, (2009). Report on Global FDI flows halved in 1st quarter of 2009, UNCTAD data show; prospects remain low for rest of year, released at press conference on 24 June, 2009, UNCTAD/PRESS/PR/2009/024, 24/06/09 http://www.unctad.org/

Templates/webflyer.asp?docid = 11666&intItemID = 1528 accessed on February 13th, 2010.

Venkatraman, N. and John E. Prescott (1990). "Environment-Strategy Coalignment: An Empirical Examination of Its Performance Implications," *Strategic Management Journal*, 11 (1), pp. 1-23.

Vorhies, D.W. and Morgan, N.A. (2003). "A Configuration Theory Assessment of Marketing Organization Fit with Business Strategy and its Relationship with Marketing Performance". *Journal of Marketing*, (67), pp. 100-115.

Vrontis, D., Thrassou, A. and Lamprianou, I. (2009). "International marketing adaptation versus standardization of multinational companies". *International Marketing Review*, 26(4/5), 477-500.

Walters, P.G.P. (1986). "International Marketing Policy: A Discussion of the Standardization Construct and its Relevance for Corporate Policy", *Journal of International Business Studies*, 17(2), pp. 55-69.

Wang, C., Yu, P., Jaw, B., and Huang, C. (2008). "Towards a cross-cultural framework of strategic international human resource control: The case of Taiwanese high-tech subsidiaries in the USA". T*he International Journal of Human Resource Management*, 19(7), 1253-1277.

Wernerfelt, B. (1984). "A resource-based view of the firm". *Strategic Management Journal*, 5 (2), pp. 171-180.

—— (1995). "The resource-based view of the firm: Ten years after". *Strategic Management Journal*, 16, pp. 171-174.

Whitelock, J. and Pimblett, C. (1997). "The Standardization Debate in International Marketing", *Journal of Global Marketing*, 10(3), pp. 45-66.

—— (1987). "Global Marketing and the Case for International Product Standardization", *European Journal of Marketing*, 21(9), pp. 32-44.

Wind, Y. (1986). "The Myth of Globalization". *Journal of Consumer Marketing*, 3 (Spring), pp. 23-26.

Won, D. (2004). "Competitive Advantage in Intercollegiate Athletics: A Resource-Based View", Unpublished dissertation presented in partial fulfillment of the requirement for the degree of doctor of philosophy, The Ohio State University.

World Trade Organization (2009). World Trade Report 2009 (accessed February 7, 2010), http://www.wto.org/english/res_e/booksp_e/anrep_e/world_trade_report09_e.pdf]

Xu, S., Cavusgil, S.T. and White, J.C. (2006). "The Impact of Strategic Fit Among Strategy, Structure, And Process On Multinational Corporation Performance: A Multimethod Assessment", *Journal of International Marketing*, 14 (2), pp. 1-31.

Yeung, H.W.C. (2008). "Transnational Corporations from Asian Developing Countries: Their Characteristics and Competitive Edge". *Journal of Asian Business*, 10(4), 17-58.

Yi, J., Zhong, Y. and Zheng, Q. (2012). "An analysis of state-owned and private-owned enterprises' export performance: The value chain perspective". *Journal of Chinese Entrepreneurship*, 4(1), 20-34.

Yip, G. (1997). "Patterns and determinants of global marketing". *Journal of Marketing Management* 13, pp. 153-164.

Yip, G.S. (2003). "Total Global Strategy II, Upper Saddle River", New Jersey: Pearson Education.

—— (1989). "Global Strategy: In a World of Nations?", *Sloan Management Review*, 31 (Fall), pp. 29-41.

—— (1995). "The Resource-Based View of the Firm: Ten Years After", *Strategic Management Journal*, 16 (3), pp. 171-174.

Young, M.A., Sauer, P.L., and Unnava, H.R. (1994). "Country-of-origin issues". In S.S. Hassan and R.D. Blackwell (Eds.), *Global marketing perspectives and cases* (pp. 196-210). Fort Worth, TX: The Dryden Press.

Zahra, S. and George, G. (2002). "Absorptive Capacity: A Review, Reconceptualization, and Extension". *Academy of Management Review*, 27, (2), pp. 185-203.

Zaiem, I and Zghidi, B. (2011). "Product Adaptation Strategy and Export Performance: The Impacts of the Internal Firm Characteristics and Business Segment". *Contemporary Management Research*, Vol. 7, No. 4 pp.

Zhou, L., Wu, A. and Barnes, B. (2012). "The Effects of Early Internationalization on Performance Outcomes in Young International Ventures: The Mediating Role of Marketing Capabilities". *Journal of International Marketing*, 20(4), 25-45.

Zou S., Fang E., and Zhao S. (2003). "The effect of export marketing capabilities on export performance: an investigation of Chinese exporter". *Journal of international marketing*, 11(4), 32-55.

—— and Fu, H. (2011). *International marketing: Emerging markets*. Bingley: Emerald Jai.

—— and Stan, S. (1998). "The determinants of export performance: A review of the empirical literature between 1987 and 1997", *International Marketing Review*, 15 (5), 333-356.

——, Kim, D. and Cavusgil, S.T. (2009). *Export marketing strategy: Tactics and skills that work*. New York, NY: Business Expert Press.

——, Taylor, C.R., and Osland, G.E. (1998). The EXPREF Scale: A Cross-National Generalized Export Performance Measure. *Journal of International Marketing*, 6(3), 37-58.

Index